LIFE IN OLD BOISE

LIFE IN OLD BOISE

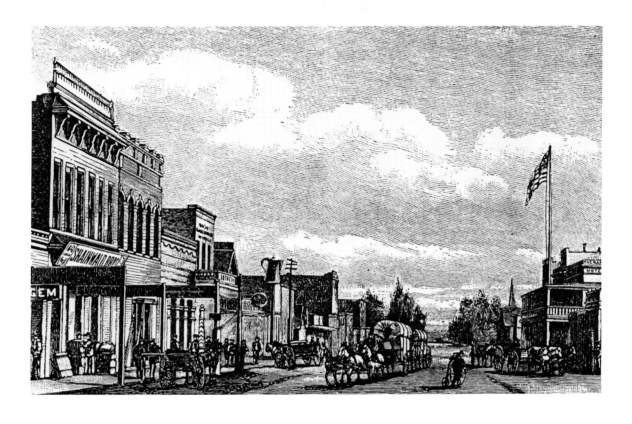

by Arthur A. Hart

Boise City Celebrations/Home Federal Savings

BOISE CITY CELEBRATIONS/HOME FEDERAL SAVINGS
Boise, Idaho
1989

Library of Congress Cataloging-in-Publication Data

Hart, Arthur A., 1921-

Life in Old Boise/Arthur A. Hart

Library of Congress Catalog Card No. 89-085146

It was a privilege for Home Federal Savings to
underwrite this beautiful book about the early days
in Boise, Idaho. All profits from its sale will be given
to Boise's Ronald McDonald House, the Boise
Senior Citizens Center and the Boise Public
Library.

I am sure you will find *Life In Old Boise* is an interesting and informative pictorial account of yester-
days in Idaho's capital city and a superbly written
book as only Arthur Hart could do.

Sincerely,

Larry B. Gates, President
Home Federal Savings

Home Federal

SERVING SOUTHERN IDAHO SINCE 1921

These engravings are from William M.
Thayer's 1887 *Marvels of the New West.*
The first, shown and described in the
book, is of Capital Square; the second is
a view of Main Street looking west from
Seventh.

CONTENTS

For Chester Edmund Cochran

FOREWORD:

 There are a thousand stories to be told about Boise and its fascinating history. Through my weekly column in *The Idaho Statesman* I have been able to tell several hundred of them. It is from these writings that the essays in this book have been selected, edited, and in some cases largely rewritten.

For the past 20 years it has been my delightful experience to read the files of old newspapers and everything else I could find about Boise. When I discover a particularly interesting story, I have the added pleasure of passing it along to my readers.

I soon learned that some of the most popular and persistent tales about the city were more fiction than fact, but that there were more than enough true stories to be discovered and retold without perpetuating the myths.

Life in Old Boise is offered as a series of vignettes that capture the flavor of people and events in Idaho's little capital city from its founding in 1863 until the 1920s. Obviously, in a book of this size no pretense is made that this is a complete or even a balanced account of Boise's history, but I think the stories selected for retelling are all interesting, all true, and all revealing of people and events that helped shape the city we know today.

Despite dramatic changes in technology over these years, human beings and human nature have remained much the same. The pioneers of Idaho wanted to make better and more secure lives for themselves and their children. When they had satisfied their basic needs for food, clothing and shelter, they aspired to something more, and gave generously to improve their community — culturally and spiritually as well as physically.

Because of its unique geographical setting, on the edge of a desert, at the foot of mountains, Boise has always enjoyed natural advantages — a stimulating climate marked by four seasons, abundant sunshine, rich soil, and water for irrigation. Access to mountains and desert has also offered recreational opportunities much appreciated and enjoyed by the people of Boise for well over a century. This is truly a special place.

Arthur A. Hart
Boise, 1989

This view of the city was published in Robert E. Strahorn's The Resources and Attractions of Idaho Territory, 1881.

An 1890 view appeared in a special holiday issue of The Idaho Statesman. *The building in center foreground, over which the artist seems to be looking, is the Central School of 1881.*

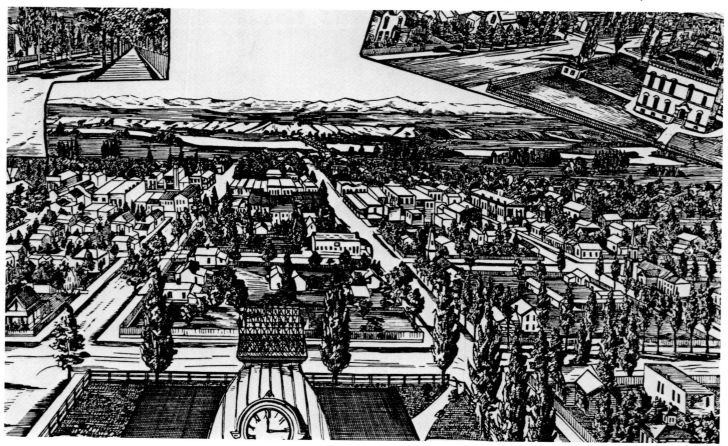

A PLEASANT SURPRISE

Since the city's founding in 1863, Boiseans have always taken a keen interest in what visitors thought of them and their town. *The Idaho Statesman* frequently reprinted in its pages descriptions of Boise City that appeared in other papers across the country. Almost always the tone of these articles was complimentary, adding to the pride citizens felt in their young community.

Washington Irving published one of the earliest descriptions of the future site of Boise in 1843 in *The Adventures of Captain Bonneville*: "The country about the Boise (or Woody) River is extolled by Captain Bonneville as the most enchanting he had seen in the Far West, presenting the mingled grandeur and beauty of mountain and plain, of bright running streams and vast grassy meadows waving to the breeze."

Bonneville remembered best a lushness that was limited to a narrow strip along the river. Most of the valley was sagebrush, even though there is evidence to indicate that the climate was in a wetter and cooler cycle then than now. (Many observers today think we are again entering such a wet cycle, as the rise in the water level of Great Salt Lake and other inland basins suggests).

John Hailey, later a founding father of the Idaho Historical Society, passed the site of Boise City on June 27, 1863, a few days before an army detachment commanded by Pinckney Lugenbeel established Fort Boise. Hailey says there were a few log cabins in the valley, but that he saw no people. "They may have been on a visit, at work, or possibly preparing for a jack rabbit drive, as the rabbits seem to be about as numerous as the sagebrush. The only growth at that time on the site of Boise was sagebrush and bunch grass, both of which grew luxuriantly."

An anonymous correspondent of *The Statesman*, who signed himself "Julius Jinks," described Boise in 1875 as "built on a plain, gradually sloping to the south, just at the foot of the hills forming the base of the Boise Mountains. Those mountains form a semi-circle, surrounding the city on the north and east. The streets are wide, and there are nice irrigating ditches running through the streets, watering beautiful forest trees which are set out with great taste. The business houses of the city are rather too low to look well."

Other visitors who published descriptions of Boise included Abigail Scott Duniway, editor of the *New Northwest* of Portland.

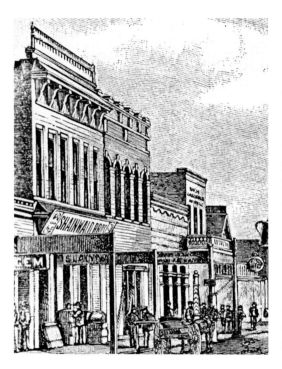

Mrs. Duniway, a pioneer advocate of women's suffrage, visited the city several times in the 19th century, speaking eloquently for her cause. *The Statesman* called her 1876 description of Boise "splendid" and praised her as "certainly the ablest lady speaker we ever heard, and we doubt if there are many men in the United States her equal."

T.F. Miner, of the *LaGrande Gazette*, wrote in 1879 that Boise was "well called 'Queen City of the Mountains.' It is making rapid strides in improvements, and its streets give one an idea of its importance among the Idahoans. In its stores, at the hotels, among the corrals, and yes, among the distributors of wet goods, all seem busy, and the appearance of the military among the citizens gives a jaunty effect that can be indulged in only by cities favored with a military garrison."

"The private residences have a clean, inviting, home-like appearance — most of them being embowered in groves of shade and fruit trees, while small fruits and shrubbery seem to grow spontaneously, undoubtedly, however, materially aided by the irrigating ditches which are met in all directions."

This photograph, taken April 25, 1901, shows
such local landmarks as the steeple of the First
Methodist church, just left of center, between
Central School and the Territorial Capitol. Ada
County Courthouse is right of the capitol and the
Columbia Theater is at far left.

English artist E. Greene made this lithographic
view of Boise City in 1883. The streets shown,
looking south, are Sixth, Seventh and Eighth.
The artist's vantage point was the new Ada
County Courthouse, completed a few months
earlier.

Boise was not too impressive a town in the 1880s, unless you had been traveling across a sagebrush desert for days (or even weeks) as many visitors had.

Most visitors to Boise in the 19th Century were surprised to find such a civilized community in the midst of a wild and unsettled country. An early historian of the West noted that "It was the common judgement of the first explorers that there was more of the strange and awful in the scenery and topography of Idaho than of the pleasing and attractive."

Little wonder, then, that later travelers who had toiled for days, or even weeks, crossing the vast, arid sagebrush plains of southern Idaho were astonished and pleased to discover a prosperous little city amid groves of trees, with attractive homes, gardens, and sparkling irrigation ditches. Boise was truly an oasis in the desert to weary emigrants who had not seen a shade tree or a house in a long time.

An 1879 visitor was impressed by the neat fences and "surroundings kept clean and tidy." He said, "One can almost imagine himself transported to some old New England town, where cleanliness and order are strictly maintained . . ."

Another aspect of Boise City that its merchants and editors always pushed was its value as a winter home for miners. Since most of the surrounding mining districts were in the mountains, and had severe winters with deep snowfall, the capital city's milder climate had an appeal. Placer miners in particular were likely to seek winter havens, since they depended upon running water to carry out their operations. From late summer until most of the snow had gone in the spring they were virtually out of business.

The *Salt Lake Tribune* extolled the virtues of Boise and her pioneers in a January 1, 1884, article. "On what was once a sagebrush plain, apparently almost a desert, such as constitutes so vast an area of Western Territory, clear sighted American grit and enterprise have within twenty years built a town which is the pride of its citizens and the admiration of strangers . . ." Commenting on Boise's healthful climate and cleanliness, the *Tribune* said that "from a sanitary point of view, the place is the admiration of everyone except the doctors and undertakers."

"In social attractions Boise is far ahead of much larger towns in the East. The lawlessness supposed to characterize so many frontier towns, is unknown here. The culture, refinement, and hospitality of the people of Boise are proverbial." Like all such extrava-

The Idaho Statesman was happy to publish all the good things visitors said about Boise through the years. This building at Sixth and Main was the paper's third location since it began printing in July, 1864.

gant praise, these comments must be viewed with a degree of skepticism, yet it is remarkable that nearly all published accounts of visits to Boise are laudatory.

One 1884 visitor to Boise called it "a model city," and the *Portland News* in that same year was equally impressed. The editor of the Sterling, Colorado, *News* visited Boise in the summer of 1885, and described it to his readers in superlatives. William M. Thayer, in his book *Marvels of the New West*, copyrighted 1887, was also impressed to find such a town in such an isolated location: "Boise City was 250 miles from the nearest railroad until three years ago, and could be reached only by a long and tiresome journey by stage or team, for days and nights. To travelers it was a desolate region, through which they journeyed to reach the little thrifty city which pluck and enterprise had reared . . . The business part of the town is built of brick and stone, a city ordinance prohibiting the erection of wooden buildings . . . There are three excellent hotels, more than twenty stores of all kinds, and three newspapers . . . The streets are wide, and so shaded with trees as to appear beautiful beyond comparison."

Boise, it seems, has long been a pleasant surprise to visitors. We think the tradition is worth continuing, and that it will be.

Julia and Thomas Jefferson Davis were married in 1871. They were pioneers in making Boise a green oasis in the desert. Davis' orchards made him a wealthy man. In 1907 he gave the city 40 acres to be used for a park in memory of his wife who died that year.

A CITY OF TREES

The name Boise, with an accent over the final "e," means "wooded" in French. The early fur trappers in this region, who were mostly from French Canada, gave the name "wood" or "wooded" to several streams in southern Idaho — streams whose cottonwood and willow groves stood out in striking and refreshing contrast to the dry sagebrush plains around.

The river had been called Boise for a long time before the town was started in July, 1863, but it would be a while before Boise City truly became a "city of trees." Even so, there were impressive and far-sighted efforts at an early date to get trees started.

Tom Davis, who eventually donated Julia Davis Park to the city, was one of the first to take up land along the river. In the spring of 1864, he planted 7,000 fruit trees, thereby establishing the orchard industry in Boise. By 1869, over a thousand of Davis' apple trees were producing fruit. Philip Ritz of Walla Walla, one of the Northwest's most prominent nurserymen, showed up in Boise in November, 1864, with a large stock of trees for sale. None of these trees could survive Boise Valley's dry climate without water for irrigation, making it a necessity to construct a system of ditches at once. *Statesman* founder and editor James S. Reynolds was an ardent advocate of both tree-planting and irrigation systems from the very beginning. He noted each advance with approval, and constantly offered advice on how the city could be made more attractive through planting. Two items from 1869 reflect the progress being made, and one of the problems:

"The tree mania prevails in this city. Almost every street is already ornamented with poplar, cottonwood, and willow trees, and as but few men are in the tree business, they observe a strict system of setting them out in a true line, and of the proper depth to make them live with a good supply of water."

"We flatter ourselves that we will be the premium or star city of the plains, when the water ditch is completed, and the street shrubbery abundantly supplied. The trees already set out make a marked change in the appearance of our city."

"We have noticed in several cases horses tied to young shade trees. The trees are entirely too young for such treatment. They are being raised at great expense and trouble. Give them a chance, and in four or five years they will be strong enough to hold horses."

Lafayette Cartee, who became surveyor general in 1867, moved to Boise that year. He became a key figure in enriching the variety of the city's trees by starting a substantial nursery on Grove Street in 1870. On 24 acres he raised plum, cherry, crab apple, quince, mulberry, black walnut, balsam fir, Norway spruce, box elder, sugar maple, and even orange trees. Later he added magnolias, lilacs, and other ornamental shrubs, trees and flowers. In those days, a substantial part of Cartee's nursery expense came from shipping costs for his stock. One order from Bloomington, Illinois, cost $176.70 for the trees, and $55.39 for postage.

Some of the most interesting and impressive trees in the city today may be seen on the grounds of the old U.S. Assay Office at 210 Main, and of the capitol. It is a far cry from 1870, when *The Statesman* could observe that "the virgin soil of capital square is innocent of a single tree, except a few scattering sage-brush."

A City of Trees

ISHS 2394

Boise orchards had real economic importance after coming of the railroad in 1883. Carloads of fruit from Tom Davis' orchards were sent regularly to Montana cities thereafter.

General Lafayette Cartee came to Idaho shortly after his wife died, leaving him with four young children to raise. He never remarried.

General Cartee

 General Lafayette Cartee was one of Boise's most active and respected community leaders. Until his death in 1891, Cartee was always in the forefront of efforts to improve his community and his state.

After a few years in Rocky Bar, he moved to Boise and became surveyor general of Idaho Territory in 1867; he was always called General Cartee thereafter.

His fame as Idaho's leading nurseryman, and his love of trees and well-kept grounds, was amusingly foreshadowed in the first newspaper ad Cartee printed in the *Idaho Tri-weekly Statesman* on Oct. 22, 1867. It read: "WARNING. I Will Positively Kill Every Hog That Breaks Into The Enclosure I Occupy. L.F. Cartee."

After opening his famous Grove Street Nursery in 1870, his ads appeared regularly for many years. News items of those years also reflect the many improvements he made on his 24 acre plot, which extended from Third Street to Fifth between Grove and Myrtle.

The trials and tribulations of getting nursery stock from the East are also reflected in a news item of April, 1871. Since the nearest railroad was at Kelton, Utah, all of the General's plants had to come to Boise from Kelton via the stagecoaches. The "boys" on the stage line were by then well-conditioned to helping out the General by soaking down his packages at every stream they crossed to keep roots and plants alive. The only trouble was, the General's package on April 13 contained drawing paper for the surveyor general's office, and the daily soaking had reduced it to a soggy mass!

Another item of that year notes that "Gen. Cartee received six sacks of mail matter by last night's coach, all of which goes into the ground of his nursery."

By 1876, the Cartee orchards were producing so well it could be reported that "Gen. Cartee has put up over five thousand cans of fruit this season. He has acres of blackberries yet, and will have tons of grapes. Who says this is not fruit country."

The General was also an active livestock breeder by 1876, with herds of cattle ranging on the Snake River many miles from Boise. He was active in all efforts to improve the quality of stock and farming methods in Idaho, and was chosen by the farmers of Ada County to lead them in their Agricultural Society in 1872. At sales of blooded stock, Cartee was often high bidder for the best animals.

As a family man and friend, Lafayette Cartee drew frequent praise through the years from those who knew him best. In August, 1871, it was reported that "Gen. Cartee, C.W. Moore, and Mr. Donaldson, with their families, left the city yesterday morning for a short stay in the mountains, and to luxuriate on game and trout." Thomas Donaldson was Register of the Land Office at the time, and later wrote one of the most valuable books of Idaho reminiscences we have. In his book "Idaho of Yesterday," Donaldson makes frequent references to Cartee, calling him a "worthy and exemplary citizen," and telling well the story of the efforts to bring the railroad to Idaho, in which both men were associated.

Like many men of wealth and culture living on the frontier, Cartee wanted better educations for his children than could be provided locally. At the same time he was supporting local efforts to secure good public schools, he sent the oldest of his three daughters to Mannheim, Germany, to study music and languages. "Miss Carrie Cartee's friends will be pleased, though not surprised, to hear that she is making very rapid progress . . ." reported the *Statesman* in 1876.

When General Lafayette Cartee's elegant Grove Street mansion was demolished shortly after the 1958 photograph shown here was taken, Boise lost a direct and tangible link with a great pioneer; she also lost an architectural treasure whose like will not come again to the local scene. Comparison with a lithograph published in San Francisco in 1878 indicates that at the time it was decided to tear it down, the Cartee house had changed little.

ISHS 1242-c

Cartee's splendid Grove Street house was long a showplace in Boise. Many visitors to the city were impressed, and wrote about it and its lush grounds. This photo was taken in the 1950s shortly before the landmark was demolished.

Lovely Grove Street was noted for its fine homes and magnificent shade trees. It took the pioneers more than thirty years of hard work and tender loving care to produce views like this one.

Beautiful Grove

 Few streets in Boise can have changed as much over the years as Grove Street. To view its treeless expanse today, one is hard put to imagine that it ever was named for its groves of trees, but so it was.

"During the long season of leaves and flowers, and of bright sunny days," wrote a visitor in 1883, "a stroll along Grove Street is like a ramble amid fields Elysian. To have a home on Grove Street is among the first and most cherished wishes of all who have ever seen the Queen of Valleys — the "Damascus of the Western Plains."

Charles A. Foster, recalling Grove Street forty years later, said "Grove Street in those days was true to its name. Large Lombardy poplars, and other varieties of shade trees adorned that thoroughfare, also made beautiful by its flower gardens and rose bushes." He went on to describe the famous Grove Street ditch along the north side of the street, with its water wheels every 50 to 100 feet.

The reputation of Grove, as the city's finest residential street, was already well established by July, 1871, when a reporter observed that "it is the Fifth Avenue of Boise City. It is inhabited by the bon ton of our society — and mosquitos."

The triumphant parading of Boise's first fire engine in 1876 also brought a mention of the thoroughfare: "Leaving the shade-embowered and rose-garlanded Edens of Grove Street, the line marched along Tenth to Main and up Main to the Engine House."

No small part of the attraction of Grove Street, when the city was very young and very small, was that the leading businessmen of Boise could live just a block from their Main Street offices. "Commencing at the foot of Fourth, and thence to the intersection of Twelfth Street, this lovely avenue is gemmed with large and beautiful private residences and Eden-like gardens and orchards.

"Prominent among these charming homes may be mentioned the residences of Gen. L.F. Cartee, John Lemp, A.G. Redway, Cyrus Jacobs, W.H. Nye, C.W. Moore, Judge H.E. Prickett, Dr. E. Smith, Frank R. Coffin, Sherman M. Coffin and others, some of which might be justly classed as magnificent in their proportions and palatial in their appointments."

This 1883 description still fit the street at the turn of the century, although a few of the city's wealthy had moved to Warm

Springs Avenue by then. Frank R. Coffin had built an even larger castle-like house on Grove in the Nineties, and the gardens were as lush as ever. In 1902 *The Statesman* ran a series of Sunday specials with photographs of the loveliest gardens in town. Grove Street still held its own.

The photographs reproduced here succeed in capturing the quality of that "lost Eden" of Boise, before the automobile and expanding commercial development had made it just a memory. At least we have the photographs and those brave old words to bring it all back.

The grandest house ever built on Grove Street was the Queen Anne mansion of Frank R. Coffin. It was completed in 1892 during the building boom that followed Idaho's admission to statehood in 1890.

ISHS 69-8.16

Christopher W. Moore's mansard-roofed house at Eight and Grove Streets was the most impressive in Idaho Territory when finished in 1879. This lithograph was published in San Francisco in 1884.

ISHS 77-22.10

Charles Ostner, sculptor of the George
Washington statue in the capitol, made the
drawing of Lafayette Cartee's house from which
this lithograph was made in San Francisco in
1878. The lacy "gingerbread" of Cartee's house
went well with the lush foliage of his Grove
Street Nursery.

*Grove Street's waterwheels lifted irrigation
water to lands above the ditch. This early photo
was taken looking west.*

Julia Davis Park had developed into a beautiful amenity for the city by the 1920s when this picture was taken. Today it is an integral link in the Boise Green Belt.

A Belt of Green

Those of us who read the old newspapers regularly, as part of our historical research, are often struck by the "rhythms of concern" that crop up from generation to generation. It is especially interesting to look back more than 80 years and to recall that Boise, even then, was much concerned about a "green belt" along the river. Many were persuaded that the city ought to take immediate steps to acquire riverfront land for park purposes.

The time was 1908. A city park system was "something that necessarily has to be spoken of in the future tense," according to a guidebook to the city published that year. There was optimism that Boise soon would have an outstanding system of parks, however, for already the Boise & Interurban electric railway company was constructing Pierce Park, four miles west of the city, and pioneer orchardist, Tom Davis, had deeded land to the city along the river for a park in memory of his wife, Julia Davis.

Pierce Park was a private enterprise, designed to entice city dwellers onto the new interurban lines that ran out State Street all the way to Middleton and Caldwell. A lake was being dug, trees planted, and rowboats were already ordered. The new park, 185 acres in extent, was named for Walter E. Pierce, the city's leading real estate developer, and a former mayor. It was a pleasant ride (especially in the open cars operated in summer) to this family picnic spot, and it grew increasingly popular in the years ahead. Today, parts of the lake, and large old trees planted then, form much of the beauty of Plantation Golf Club.

Julia Davis Park was then an undeveloped tract of land 33 acres in extent, that had been part of Tom Davis' pioneer fruit farm. In 1908, it was open grassy meadowland fringed with a few native cottonwood trees.

Recognizing the need to protect the riverfront, and that Boise had never planned for any parks in the past, there was a widespread movement to secure a "green belt," extending from the park at Broadway, to the Natatorium — a distance of two more miles. This would have made a continuous river bank park of over three miles. There were further plans to build "a beautiful boulevard" from the eastern end of the park, over to the foothills, and thence back westward to connect with the new Harrison Boulevard. This route would "skirt the hills," providing a sort of by-pass, as well as a scenic drive along the north edge of town.

NO.1. BOAT HOUSE, COUNTRY CLUB, BOISE, IDAHO.

Pierce Park, site of today's Plantation Golf Club, was a delightful recreational spot in the city's streetcar era. Boating on artificial lakes like this one was popular, as were picnicking and dancing. The park was built by the interurban company.

A $100,000 bond issue was to be voted upon on June 29, 1908, to see if Boise would acquire and develop the riverfront extension east of the land Tom Davis had given. A spirited campaign occupied the attention of Boiseans for two months prior to the election. Band concerts, free streetcar rides, and other inducements were offered to get the people out to see the proposed "green belt" area, and many hundreds turned out on weekends.

Several leading citizens, including banker C.W. Moore, said they had been skeptical until they actually walked over the area and realized its unique beauty and suitability for park development. *The Statesman* supported the project, and placed whole pages at the disposal of community leaders who wished to make statements pro or con.

The vote, when it came, was a decisive defeat for the park. 752 voted against the bond issue, 498 for it. Fear of increased taxes and disagreement over the particular parcel of land, were given as reasons for the defeat. Some had favored city purchase of land downstream from the Davis tract.

Mayor John Haines, who had thought the bond issue a wise investment, now announced: "During the remainder of my administration the matter of securing city parks will not be taken up or considered in any form."

The Statesman also recognized that the people had spoken, but pointed out that "it is not unreasonable to assume that at some future time our people will have cause to regret their action on Monday." With the wisdom of hindsight, many now noted that this land could once have been acquired for the city for a few dollars an acre, and that the chances were it would cost far more in the future than in the "missed chance" of 1908.

Flowers in the Desert

Garden seeds were part of the cargo emigrants stowed carefully into their covered wagons when they headed west. Farmers would need to plant crops as soon as they could. Their wives would need vegetable gardens to supply the family table.

Sentiment surely played a part in the choice of what to bring, and most women brought along packets of flower seeds from the homes they left behind. Hollyhocks, Sweet Williams, Canterbury Bells, Asters, Foxglove, and Bee Balm would help to make the new place seem like home.

Southern Idaho's desert climate presented a real challenge to the pioneers, most of them from the East or Midwest, where summer rainfall was abundant. They had to learn irrigation agriculture, and a whole new way of growing things. There were ditches and wells to dig, trees to plant for shade and windbreaks. Watering often had to be done by hand, sometimes on a daily basis.

Although making a living came first, it is evident that flowers and ornamental trees and shrubs were planted very early in Idaho frontier towns and farmyards. To make the sagebrush deserts seem like home took time and effort. The job then was what it still is today in new housing developments: to create mini-environments in which a wide variety of plants could grow. Shade and moisture-loving species needed shelter from the hot summer sun and drying winds. Soil conditions had to be altered to take into account plants that needed more or less acidity to do well.

Although folk wisdom, rather than science, guided the early settlers in their creation of special growing conditions, there were soon dealers in plants on the frontier and agricultural societies where knowledge and experience could be shared. Lafayette Cartee, for example, a civil engineer with a scientific turn of mind, operated the Grove Street Nursery in Boise City for a generation. He imported thousands of fruit and shade trees, ornamental shrubs, berries, and flowering plants to supply farmers and town dwellers alike.

Cartee's own place, at Fourth and Grove Streets, was a show place. In 1872 *The Statesman* said that his "grounds and improvements surpass anything this side of California." The fame of Cartee's gardens and nursery spread far and wide. *The Owyhee Avalanche* of Silver City published a lengthy and laudatory description of the place in 1877, and in October, 1878, Portland's *West Shore Magazine* printed a description and lithographic view.

That Boiseans took great pride in creating a "new Eden" in the desert is suggested by dozens of newspaper references through the years, to landscaping, trees, shrubs, and flower gardens. That love of gardens continues to the present.

ISHS 73-190.5/a

Warm Springs Avenue became the city's showplace after 1890 when hot wells were drilled, the Natatorium was built, and streetcars began to run there. Its gardens were showplaces.

THE SEASONS

Cooling Camps

The cool breezes and pine-scented air of Idaho's mountains have attracted Boise campers for well over a century. To those living on southern Idaho's sagebrush plains where summers are warm, the tantalizing sight of the mountains on both northern and southern horizons has long been hard to resist.

"Rusticating," as it was called then, entailed considerably more preparation and planning than a similar trip does today. Equally important with human needs for the trip were the needs of the horses who would get the campers to their chosen retreat and back again.

These items from an account book of the 1870s give modern readers an idea of what was needed for even short trips: shoeing the horses, sacks of oats, hay, cups of axle grease, and even a gallon of castor oil. The need for a whole gallon of this noxious stuff, which was the terror of childhood existence in those days, is a mystery. It could have been used on the horses, or even as harness oil, but no one we have talked to knows for sure.

Once the family was encamped, the pursuit of fish and game became the principal occupation of the men. Grouse were favored for variety from the trout which made up the bulk of mountain meals, but our old account book also lists fifteen pounds of dried apples, coffee, sugar, bacon, and one gallon of whiskey. (The price was three dollars and a half.) One hundred cigars and one pound of candles are also included in this interesting record of a trip from Boise.

Game laws were lax and enforcement almost unknown. Most accounts of those early camping trips which got to the newspapers resemble this one of 1876: "Messrs. Thomas E. Logan, Thomas Ranney, and William E. Nye, returned on Tuesday from their fishing excursion on Canyon Creek, which is about thirty miles from the city . . . they caught seven hundred beautiful and delicious trout, which they generously distributed among their friends in the city."

On a similar week-long outing in 1872, it was reported that Logan and friends, including several ladies, "caught about 15,000, though it was impossible to keep a strict account." This was most likely a "fish story," but the catches were certainly unrestricted.

In the Eighties, Shafer Creek was a popular place for groups of

ISHS 74-50.39

Judge Fremont Wood's family camped out on Payette Lakes around the turn of the century. The lakes have been a popular summer resort for Boiseans for well over a century.

An aspen campsite in Idaho's mountains. The family came by the wagon in the background, hence had to provide for horses as well as people on any extended outing.

campers from the valley, especially in August. Businessmen would get their families settled into a comfortable spot and commute to the city every few days. It was part of the fun for two or more families to share a location: "The party there now have three canvas tents and a shadowy bower of fir boughs where 'tired nature's sweet restorer' overtakes the drooping eyelids and wraps the sleeper in such repose as house-dwellers never can know," wrote a visitor in 1881.

Camps on Shafer Creek in 1882 were given names and decorated with flags. *Germany* was shared by the families of John Lemp and William Jaumann, *Brooklyn* by the Brodbecks and Bilderbacks, *New York* by the Post, Dausman, and Cohn families. John Lawrence called his campsite *American Flat*, perhaps for contrast to his largely German-speaking neighbors on the creek.

By the early Nineties, Payette Lakes were being visited regularly for the summer by campers from the valley. As yet there were only a few mountain locations which offered lodging, so camping was the rule, although Idaho City drew its share of summer visitors who put up at the Luna House of Matthew G. Luney. Then, as now, Idahoans had the blessing of a mountain retreat not far away — even by horse and wagon.

Several families often camped together, extending the social life of the city to the cool camps of higher altitudes.

ISHS 1158-36

Idle crowds of men like these irritated Statesman *editor James S. Reynolds. They hung out in favorite saloons like that of James Lawrence and Madison Smith until spring thaws made placer mining in the hills profitable again.*

Why Stand Ye Idle?

Although Boise depended upon the trade that miners brought to local merchants in the winter, when water was frozen in the higher elevations and placering came to a halt, the presence of all of these idle men sometimes got on the nerves of townspeople and editors. Boise was always glad to see them come in the fall, but just as glad to see them leave in the spring!

Statesman Editor James S. Reynolds was particularly out of patience with the miners who hung around Boise's Main Street saloons in the spring of 1870. He never missed a chance that year to chide the loafers for not going out early and at least trying to make an honest dollar. We are forced to speculate that a good many of these men were living on the cuff by spring, and that their creditors were eager to see them go to work.

In February, Reynolds tried to stir up a little action by noting that a large number of whites and Chinese had been working the bars of Boise River with rockers all winter, in an area six miles long below the mouth of More's Creek, "some of them making good wages, others indifferent, but the poorest of them doing better than lying idle." He also reported that 800 men were expected to make from $4 to $10 a day each in the Wagontown Diggings, which extended for 12 miles along Jordan Creek below Silver City.

On March 1, the editor inserted the needle again: "A man was in town on Sunday with quite a lot of gold dust taken from the claims on the river a few miles above town. Men do not want to work very much when they remain idle where good wages can be easily made a short distance up the river. Stand in, men and go to taking out gold dust. Why stand ye idle?"

Later that month came reports of activity on Snake River below Shoshone Falls. Again, editor Reynolds tried to stir up action by optimistic reports on what was going on there. Although he stated that men were making "very good wages" with rockers, the Snake Rive gold was so fine as to be very difficult to recover. The elusive "flour gold" of the Snake River placers attracted a real rush in the spring of 1870, due in part, no doubt, to James Reynolds' editorializing.

On April 16, *The Statesman* reported "The spring rush toward the mines has occasioned quite a demand for horseflesh. A brisk trade in horses has been going on for several days." On April 26,

Miners were a rough and ready crowd who regularly came out of the hills in the fall to winter in places like Boise City where the climate was milder.

in another outburst of optimism, it was said that several hundred men were engaged in the placering on Snake River, "and from eight to $25 per day to the hand are taken out. The gold is very fine, requiring a large amount of quicksilver to save it."

Finally, on April 28, the editor crusading against sloth wrote with obvious satisfaction: "The crowd of idle men who daily filled our streets some days ago has dispersed — all gone to the different mining camps to work."

But, as is often the case with having our wishes fulfilled, editor Reynolds lamented in July that the rush to the Snake River mines had caused a serious shortage of laboring men, especially farm hands. He also had to report that the exodus had been premature, as the waters of the Snake were still too high for working the bars, and advised waiting until August to migrate. By July, Reynolds had also revised his estimate of the money to be made daily to "fair wages — $4-$5 per day."

Jingle Bells in Boise

"Dashing through the snow, in a one-horse open sleigh" are just the words of an old song to most of us today, but it was once a popular part of life in Boise.

Often in snowy winters, it was necessary to take to the runners just to get around, and even stagecoaches and wagons were converted to them. Just as often, however, people who owned the graceful "cutters" of the day, went sleigh riding for the sheer pleasure of it, and lamented a winter too mild to enjoy a favorite winter sport.

The winter of 1865 was always remembered with fondness by old-timers as the best sleighing season Boise ever had. Later snowy winters were always compared with that one. 1872 offered a short February season much enjoyed by all: "The snow began to fall on Saturday and continued nearly all day and most of Sunday," wrote *The Statesman*. . . . "We have almost six inches, and the sleigh bells are jingling around town in a lively way. It is good for those that have time to enjoy the sport, but the appearance is the beautiful snow will not last long." This prediction was borne out a few days later, when it was reported that C.W. Moore, Cy Jacobs, and Austin Savage had to walk five or six miles up the canyon of Boise River to find enough snow to continue their sleigh ride to Idaho City.

Stagecoaches had the same problem. Wheels had to be replaced with runners, and then back again, as changing road conditions shortened the tempers of drivers. Passengers often had to get out and walk — but it was all an accepted part of winter travel in a pioneer country.

"Whirling Through Snow Go Happy Boise Crowds" was the headline on an 1898 story about one of Boise's premier sleighing seasons. "It is a strange statement to make in a mountainous section," wrote *The Statesman*, "but it is nevertheless true that sleighing is a decided rarity in Boise . . ."

"Since the first appreciable fall of snow on the frozen ground, the merry jingle of bells has been heard all day and until far into the night. Every cutter has been pressed into service, the liverymen are reaping a harvest, and their animals are reaping a retirement on full feed . . . no street but rings with the gleeful shouts of riders, and country runs are being taken advantage of. Every form of sleigh is seen, and none so poor he cannot enjoy the fun. Wheels are removed, and iron often of grotesque shape substituted, while some outfits consist of store boxes mounted on plain wooden runners, and mules and even dogs are drafted into service.

"For the boys it is a period of unalloyed enjoyment and doctor nor undertaker for them have no terrors if they can but 'hook on' and speed like the wind. Prospects of broken limbs or whooping cough and the wrath of spoony sleighers restrain them not."

The French poet Francois Villon asked, more than 500 years ago, "but where are the snows of yesterday?" Some of them, at least, can be made real again by reading the pages of Idaho newspapers. How delightful it is to discover that Boise's Boys' Band drove through the streets in that great snow of 1898, and "filled the air with their music," and that the merry crowds following in sleighs took up the refrain. Perhaps in anticipation of a thaw they whooped up, "There'll Be A Hot Time in the Old Town Tonight."

Christmas Past

Christmas trees had been in use in America for about a generation when Idaho was settled, and little old Boise City knew them from its first days. It was the custom of the 1860s to have community trees in Boise, rather than individual ones in homes. For one thing, the nearest evergreens were on top of Boise Front, several miles from the town at its foot. For most families, it was just too much work to climb to the snowy foothills to get a tree for the living room.

In 1865 Boise City's only Sunday school supplied the community tree. Since there weren't many halls in town big enough for a Christmas concert and party, the room rented by the Territorial Legislative Assembly in the store building of May & Brown was used.

"The Christmas Tree will be free to all who wish to communicate through it with their friends," said *The Statesman*, and announced that a committee would receive gifts for the tree from two until four on Christmas Eve. The party started at six, and was open to the public. Children furnished the music, and the reporter was impressed by one "little Miss" who sang, "If I Were a Sunbeam."

Meanwhile, at Fort Boise the officers gave a "sociable" for the townspeople. Fifty couples enjoyed a gourmet supper and danced "until daylight peeped over the hills." Although there was apparently no Christmas tree present, "the spacious hall was brilliantly illuminated and tastefully decorated with flags and evergreens, and at either end large fireplaces piled with blazing fir wood gave it the appearance and air of comfort rarely seen outside of a New England sitting room."

In 1866 the community had two parties featuring Christmas trees. This time it was the hall of the Territorial House of Representatives in Hart's Exchange Hotel that was chosen for the occasion by the Baptist Sunday School.

It is interesting that the House adjourned "at an early hour" specifically to make way for the Sunday school party. The Episcopalians, who had a brand new church of their own, held their Christmas tree party in the handsome Gothic Revival building, now called Christ Chapel, located near Broadway bridge on the BSU campus.

The following night a public Christmas Ball was held in Hart's Exchange. Tickets were "ten dollars currency" (no gold dust,

ISHS 2-c

Community Christmas parties were usually held in the churches in early Boise. This is how St. Michael's Episcopal church was decorated for Christmas in 1870. This building is now Christ Chapel on the campus of Boise State University.

please), and an ad promised that the "finest music in the territory" would be in attendance. Ladies and gentlemen "tripped the light fantastic until near the hour for breakfast," said the report in the paper's next issue, and the writer urged continuance of a pleasant development at the party: "That idea of introducing songs while waiting for supper is a good one. Boys, you that are singists, why don't you organize a quartet, or glee-club?"

The Baptists were still celebrating for the children with a tree in 1868, as a Christmas Eve story of that year tells us: "The Christmas tree now growing in the Baptist Church will shed its fruit at six o'clock this evening. Do not forget to graft something on one of its boughs for the little folks."

Leap Year Lasses

Leap Year has been noted and celebrated in Idaho since the Territory was founded. Today's customs being what they are, there is less and less novelty in having women assume a more aggressive role in courting than there was a century, or even a generation ago.

Young women in Nineteenth Century Idaho, however, actually could work up quite a case of "butterflies in the tummy" at the thought of daring to ask a young man to a party or a dance.

There is ample evidence in old accounts that, butterflies or not, the girls loved the freedom Leap Year gave them to reverse the social roles. From the earliest days in January, young women (and their mothers) were busy planning parties and sociables where "ladies' choice" could operate freely.

In 1876, a grand New Year's party, "Leap Year style," was held in which the local belles reversed the usual procedures with great consistency, even calling for their young men in sleighs, taking their wraps, escorting them into the ballroom, and bringing them glasses of punch.

They also took advantage of the occasion to make a point, leaving their partners stranded and disconsolate for one protracted period while they pretended to go out for a surreptitious whisky — apparently a male custom at early Idaho dances. The boys got the point, alright, but whether it improved their manners is open to question.

A long account of another New Year's party that year came down from Fairview, describing the gay festivities in the little mining town on the side of War Eagle mountain near Silver City.

Kittle's Hall and Toy's Hotel were the scene of heart-warming gaiety in the midst of the deep mountain snows. Fairview had suffered a fire in October that virtually wiped out the town, but was back in business by January. Today, only a few miners' cabins amid the rocks nearby mark Fairview's location, although there is a cemetery below the townsite. The great hulk of the Cumberland Mill, built later, survived until torched this year.

In 1872, *The Statesman* published a poem entitled "Leap Year, 1872," in which local bachelors were sorted and classified by a young woman in a quandary:

"I'm in doubt. I'm in doubt, whom shall I pity
Of all the bachelors in Boise City?
Whom shall I ask to share household and purse?

ISHS 65-70.8

Charming young women like these displayed their charms and fanciest hats at a variety of special leap year activities.

45

Eligible young bachelors of Boise in the 1870s were treated royally during leap year festivities. At parties they behaved well, but as one wit pointed out, "it was not always a dry well."

Whom shall I take 'for better for worse'?''
A sample taken from the ten-stanza epic, reads as follows:
"Bilderback, Roth, Schwabacher, and Falk,
Lean over the counter and deal in small talk;
Frank Coffin is jolly, but it's horrid to know
That the day I was married to my Coffin I'd go.''

The short physical descriptions of some of these bachelors constitute the only surviving record of what they looked like, since no photographs of them can be found. Several are listed as too short, too fat, or too tall.

While some old bachelors liked it that way, there were others who viewed leap year with a faint springing of hope. Tom Morrow, Boise City Marshal, said he would marry the first woman who proposed, "just to give the boys a chance to toot their horns."

Another, writing of Leap Year and its prospects, characterized "those lonely specimens of the genus bachelor," so frequently found in Idaho mining camps, as like himself, "wishing for every woman they see, and enjoying possession of none."

We hope some young lady took pity on the poor fellow.

Our Fair Queen

One of the most beloved of American institutions is the county fair, and Boise was not long in starting its own fairs, once agriculture was well established.

Traditionally, rural fairs have consisted of exhibits of livestock, farm produce, and crafts, but there has also been a wide range of more active entertainments. In the 19th century, when the horse dominated Idaho transportation, racing meets were well attended as annual week long events, before becoming part of the fairs, and it was not until 1897 that the first really big and comprehensive fair was held in southwest Idaho.

Mayor Moses Alexander proclaimed the First Idaho Intermountain Fair on October 9, 1897, to run from the 12th to the 16th of that month. This first of many Intermountain Fairs was held at Agricultural Park, south of State Street, beyond 20th. Since this was west of the city and beyond the end of the streetcar line, people had to get there on foot, horseback, or in horse-drawn vehicles.

Bessie Vollmer, daughter of Lewiston's wealthiest merchant, was chosen queen of the first fair. Votes cost ten cents each, and were sold to raise funds for the fair, as well as to insure a lively interest in the choice of a queen. Since Bessie was undeniably an attractive young woman, her election was probably a reflection of Lewiston's pride in outdoing Boise, as much as of her father's wealth.

It is a delight to read the list of events at that first big fair: a volunteer firemen's hose race, bicycle races, concerts by the town bands of Boise, Pocatello and DeLamar, a big parade (featuring Queen Bess escorted by 100 mounted "cowboys"), and a grand ball at the Natatorium later in the evening.

Horse racing supplied most of the interest at the fairgrounds, for several boxcars of thoroughbreds from Montana and Oregon had come to compete with Idaho's fastest. A unique parade feature was the contingent of Boise butchers who marched in their white aprons and straw hats, with meat cleavers in hand.

Temporary "pavilions" were erected at the fairgrounds in each of the first few years. In 1898 it was called a "white city in miniature," after the great Chicago Fair of five years earlier. An interesting feature of the 1898 fair was a "pioneer department" for the display of relics of early days. W.C. Tatro, an old-time stage line operator, collected together "the first whipsaw, the first mowers,

"Remarkably beautiful" is the way The Idaho
Statesman *described Minnie Finnegan, queen of
the Third Idaho Intermountain Fair of 1899.*

and the first plow" for the occasion.

As the years went by, the competition for Queen of the Fair remained intense. At the Third Idaho Intermountain Fair of 1899, Minnie Finnegan of Boise was chosen for the honor. *The Statesman* noted that "she is of queenly bearing and is remarkably beautiful." Reporters delighted in the play of words when they could call her "our fair queen," and were surprised to discover that Queen Minnie was a fine watercolor painter. Two of her efforts may be seen on the walls of the Idaho Historical Museum's Victorian Parlor — interesting reminders of the charm of the Nineties.

ISHS 552-a

Queen Minnie, right, and attendants Rebecca Hays and Theresa O'Farrell rode to the fairgrounds in style in this elegant open carriage. The fair was held on September 25-26, 1899.

This turn-of-the-century view shows sideshow and carnival row at the Idaho Intermountain Fair.

In 1904 everybody came to Boise's fairgrounds on the bench (near present Orchard and Fairview) by horse and buggy.

PILLARS OF SOCIETY

These pioneer leaders of Boise City included
Statesman *editor James Reynolds, seated at far*
right, Lafayette Cartee, seated far left, and
Territorial Governor David Ballard, standing, in
center. All were prominent Republicans at a
time when most Idahoans were southern
Democrats.

Founding Father

 He, more than any other man, created Idaho's capital city. He laid it out, he got the legislation passed to make it capital, and he later got it made into an incorporated village. He even created the county in which it is located, by introducing and securing passage of the necessary legislation. When they wanted to name the new county after him, he modestly declined. His friends saw to it that the new entity was named after his young daughter, Ada, instead.

Henry Chiles Riggs had named his first son Cache, after the California town of Cacheville where the family lived when he was born. Cache died in infancy, but another son, Henry Chiles Riggs, Jr., was to carry on the family tradition of geographical names. (He named a son Boise Green Riggs, and also had a grandson of that name.) Henry senior named his last child Idaho May Riggs. Ada Hobbs Riggs reversed the usual process when Ada County was named for her. (Ada Hobbs Riggs Coon died May 29, 1909, at San Francisco.)

Kentucky native H.C. Riggs' long and adventurous career included active service in the Mexican War, 1846-47, during which time he was a scout; a trip across the continent to the California gold fields in 1850, a return trip by sea around Cape Horn, and another trip across the plains to California with a new bride in 1854. In California, Riggs held his first political job as a commissioner of Yolo County. After he moved to Corvallis, Oregon, a few years later, he was rewarded for his gifts by being elected mayor in 1861.

When news of the Idaho gold rush and its prospects were widely circulated, Riggs again decided to move. On July 6, 1863, just three days after Pinckney Lugenbeel and his army detachment had selected a site for Fort Boise, Riggs pitched his tent in what is now Boise City.

Riggs' popularity wherever he went is reflected by the fact that his new friends in Boise Valley got him appointed county judge, although he never qualified for the position. A few months later he was elected a Boise County representative to the Territorial Legislature meeting at Lewiston. This turned out to be a good move for southern Idaho's interests, but bad news for Lewiston. At that Second Session of the Idaho Legislature Riggs introduced and fought through two significant bills.

The first moved the capital to Boise City, center of the new min-

Henry Chiles Riggs was a founding father of Boise City, led the fight to have it made capital of Idaho Territory, and helped create Ada County.

Ada Hobbs Riggs, for whom Ada County is named. Her father, H.C. Riggs, engineered removal of the capital from Lewiston to Boise in 1864, and formation of the new county, named for his 8 year old daughter in his honor. Ada lived most of her life in San Francisco.

ISHS 61-96.5

ing population, and the second created a new county in the vicinity of the town. It was at this time that his friends wanted to call the new county Riggs, and ended up naming it Ada, instead.

"It is doubtful if any other man could have accomplished so much for his constituents at this session as has Mr. Riggs," commented *The Statesman* on January 10, 1865. "No fraud, no trick, no device was left untried to defeat the just measures in behalf of this portion of the territory, introduced by him and fought to a successful issue. To accomplish them under such circumstances requires not only the highest order of talent, but a clearness that no attack can surprise and industry that no opposition can tire."

H.C. Riggs died at Boise on July 3, 1909, nearly 46 years to the day after he arrived there and began to put the place on the map.

Boise Green Riggs, Sr., son of H.C. Riggs, Jr., carried on the family tradition of geographical names. He had a son Boise, and an Aunt Idaho.

High Society

Boise City in the 1890s had a kind of social aristocracy modeled after that of larger cities in the eastern states. To think that this local "high society" was typical of all of Boise of that day would, of course, be a mistake, but to think of its members as wealthy snobs who had inherited their money is equally misguided.

Although a few of Boise's leading merchants had brought modest capital with them when they arrived, most had achieved financial success and social status "the old fashioned way — they had earned it."

Like the children of every generation that prospers, Boise's young people were the beneficiaries of their parents' hard work. Life for the boys and girls that lived on Grove Street or Warm Springs Avenue was spiced by a year-round cycle of parties, picnics and dances.

Many would have agreed with Leona Hailey Cartee, daughter of pioneer stageline operator John Hailey, that Grove Street in her childhood was "the prettiest street in Boise." She recalled that her mother's generation were happy women who were spared household drudgery because they had Chinese cooks, gardeners and laundrymen who did all of that. Looking back many years later, Leona remembered Grove Street as "a picture of quiet and restful life. In fact, there seemed to be a general impression that to live on Grove Street, and belong to the Episcopal Church was all that was necessary to open the doors of good society, and unbar the gates of heaven."

The "doors of good society" in Boise City were open not only to Episcopalians, however. The little city in the sagebrush was remarkably democratic and cosmopolitan, valuing integrity, personality and pioneer accomplishment above mere wealth. Boise's social circles included a high proportion of Roman Catholics and Jews, along with Protestants.

Intermarriage between religions was generally frowned upon and rare, but the young people of all groups attended parties and dances together regularly in the 1890s and after. We learn this from the guest lists published in *The Idaho Statesman* society pages in those years. The daughter of a Jewish merchant, of a German Catholic brewer, and of an Episcopal farmer, each had her turn as the belle of young Boise society.

Fashionable dress was part of Boise's social scene in the 1890s

ISHS 76-138.19

These Boise youngsters were among the city's earliest tennis players. Margaret Cobb, at right, was the daughter of Calvin Cobb, publisher of The Idaho Statesman — *a job she herself would later inherit.*

The front steps of the elegant new home of Tom and Julia Davis on Seventh Street (later Capitol Boulevard) was the setting for this 1890s group, described in the text.

and young men were as fastidious as their girl friends in sporting the latest styles. The charming photograph reproduced here, illustrates the point. High collars and bow ties were the thing that season, and all of the gay blades in our picture are wearing them. Although one lad wears a billed cap, the rest have straw "skimmers."

Straw hats with flat crowns were "in" for the girls that season, too, and only beautiful Bella Falk, upper left, wears a flowered creation. Her sister, Anne, far right, has a skimmer. The Branstetter sisters, Alice and Dolly, are front row center with white parasols. (Freckles and tans were *not* considered attractive in those days, and young ladies guarded their fair skins in summer.)

This photo was posed on the steps of the Thomas Jefferson Davis house that once faced Julia Davis Park on Capitol Boulevard. Tom and Julia's daughter Etta is the vivacious young lady, top center, eyeing Oden Athey. The other young men are Hugh Pettengill, Otto Burns, Louis Stark and Clyde Ustick. The same group posed for a series of other charming photographs that summer — pictures that give us the flavor of the carefree life of some Boise teenagers in the Gay Nineties.

Not all Boise children were as well off as those who lived on Grove Street. The Idaho Childrens Home on Warm Springs Avenue supported many underprivileged young people. Some, as this picture shows, did not have shoes. Cynthia Mann, left, long an outstanding Boise teacher, was one of the home's founders.

ISHS 2024

Handsome young attorney William E. Borah was newly arrived in Boise City when he posed with a friend for this portrait. For some reason he holds a cavalry saber in his hand.

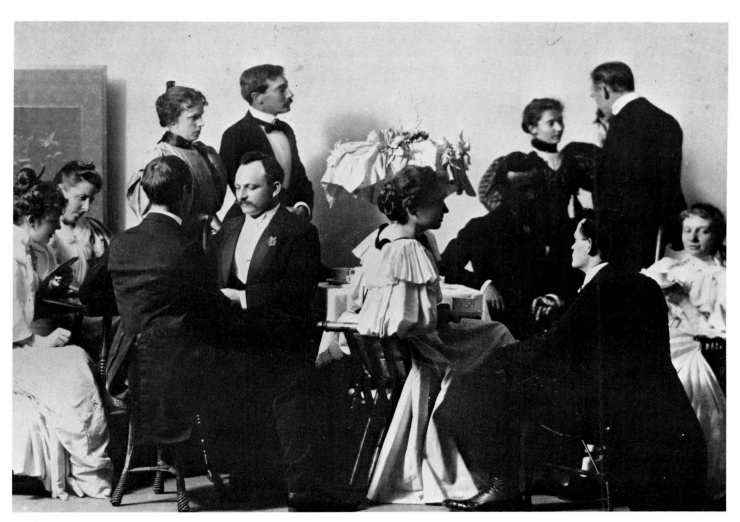

70-170.3

Whist was a popular game among Boise's social elite in the Nineties. This group were members of the city's first Whist Club. Bridge would replace it later, and is still a favorite recreation of many.

Dancing was a favorite recreation of Boiseans from the beginning. This charming Mary Hallock Foote drawing shows the skill that enabled her to publish and illustrate her own stories for a national audience.

Mary Hallock Foote published stories and drawings in national magazines like Century *while living in a canyon home east of the city in the 1880s. She and her engineer husband Arthur D. Foote later had a ranch on the site of present Hillcrest Country Club.*

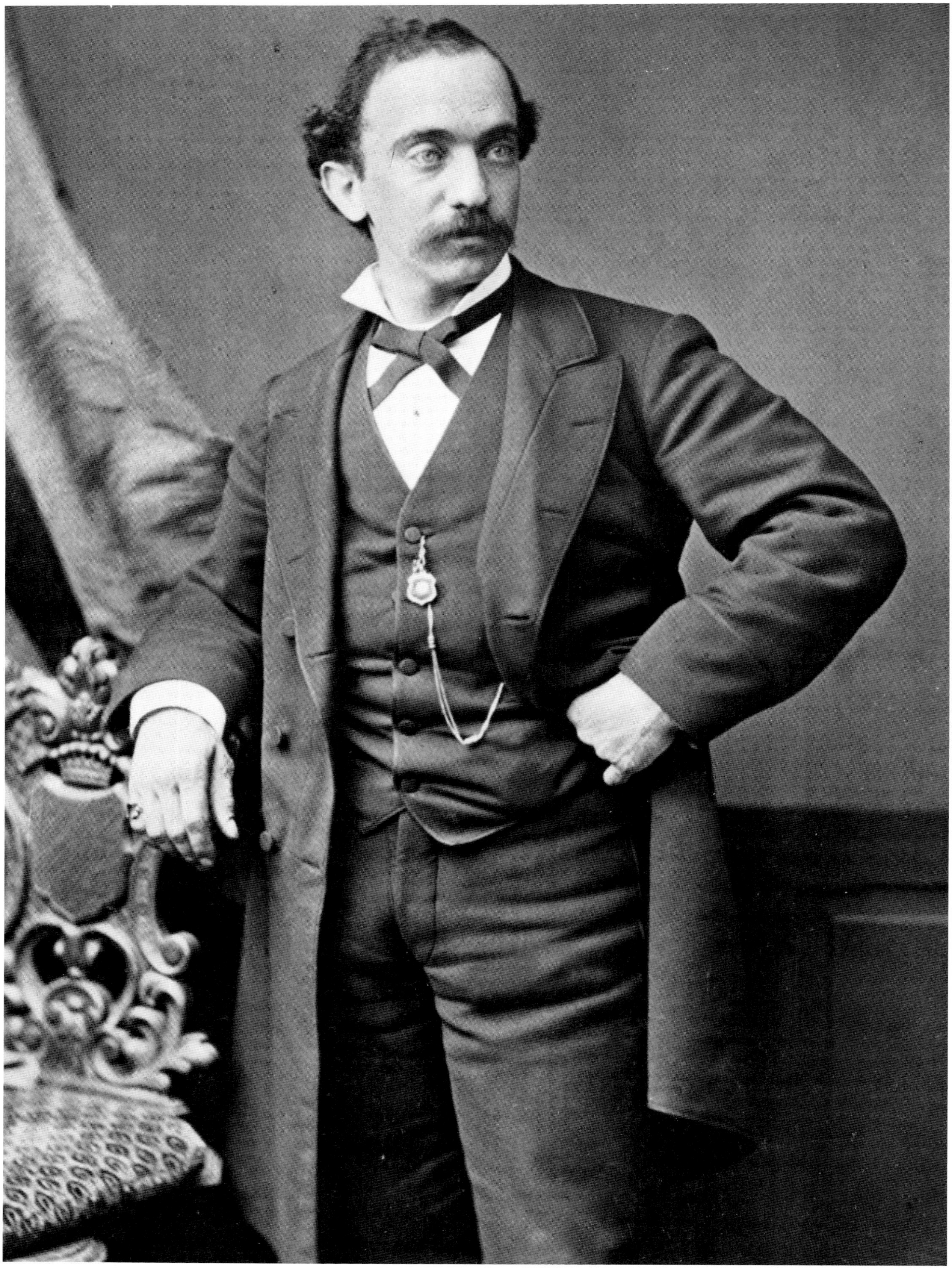

ISHS 73-20.16

Nathan Falk

"By the untimely death of Nathan Falk this city and the state of Idaho sustain a loss so great that it seems almost irreparable." Those words from a *Statesman* editorial on July 23, 1903, suggest the importance to his community of the pioneer Boise merchant who had completed his turreted Warm Springs Avenue mansion only a few months before. Falk was in Hailey on business when he was stricken with the illness that took his life a week later.

Nathan Falk was born on July 12, 1847, in Eggenhausen, Bavaria, and educated in Germany and France. He came to America when he was 15, and arrived in Boise in 1865 when only 18. His brother David, ten years his senior, had arrived the year before, and was in business with Hessberg & Co. When David Falk bought out Hessberg, his younger brother joined him to form in 1868 D. Falk & Brother, located at the northeast corner of Eighth and Main for more than a century. A branch store in Payette Valley operated by the firm for a few years, gave its name to the post office of Falk's Store, not far from Emmett.

The Falk brothers included Sigmund, who served as United States vice consul in Munich from 1899 until 1901. All of the family maintained close personal ties with their ancestral homeland throughout their lives. Nathan Falk went to Germany in 1878 to marry Miss Rose Steinmeier. They had six children, Bella, Anna, Leo, Ralph, Harry and Theodore.

Fellow pioneers were shocked at the death of Nathan Falk, for many of Boise's leading citizens had known him for nearly forty years. Frank R. Coffin recalled that they had both come to Boise in 1865, that Falk had gone into business in 1868, and Coffin in 1870, and that they had reminisced about the old days the last time they met. In 1903, the two old friends were the last from those days still in business on Main Street. "He was a noble and generous friend," wrote Coffin, "a public spirited and unselfish citizen."

"Into that beautiful home, lovingly erected by him to shelter his devoted invalid wife and loving children, a great and overwhelming grief has entered . . . May the grasses grow green, and the flowers bloom sweetly above his ashes forever. Old friend and neighbor, Hail and Farewell."

Mayor James Hawley, another pioneer of 1865, said "He was a loyal, progressive citizen, a man whose personality appealed to

ISHS 73-20.13

The family of Rose and Nathan Falk was prominent in Boise civic, business and social circles. Son Leo, far right, would build the Owyhee Hotel and the Egyptian Theater.

all classes, and whose purse was ever open when money was needed for a good purpose . . . he was a public benefactor in every sense of the word, and by his death every citizen of Boise has lost a friend."

Peter Sonna, another old-time merchant and former mayor, said that Falk was "wonderfully well liked" and "one of the most enterprising men I ever met." Bishop Glorieux added his eulogy to the others: "He was a man of sound judgment and the very soul of honor. Boise can ill afford to lose such a citizen. I feel that I have lost a dear friend and counselor . . ."

Nathan Falk, like other Jewish pioneers, deserves to be remembered as one of the builders of Boise, and of Idaho. His descendents continue the tradition of leadership and enterprise that he established.

This interior view of Nathan Falk's Queen Anne style mansion at 139 Warm Springs Avenue was taken on the occasion of a family wedding. It records the elegant gifts received. The Falk dining room can be seen in the Idaho Historical Museum where it was restored after the house was demolished in 1970.

Main Street in the 1880s was lined with saloons. John Lemp owned several and supplied a number of others from his brewery, located between Third and Fourth Streets on Main.

Lagered by Lemp

One of Idaho's most popular men in pioneer days was also one of her wealthiest. The two attributes do not always go hand in hand, but brewer John Lemp had unique and appealing qualities his friends found irresistible. Stories of his early days shed some light on both his social and financial success:

The Idaho Tri-weekly Statesman, January 6, 1870: "Lagered. — John Lemp, of the Boise Brewery, unlimbered his caisson in front of this office the other day, and stormed the boys with a keg of his best brew. The keg is now empty. John remembers his friends during the holidays, and they all hope he will brew his beer for many a day yet to come."

Idaho Tri-weekly Statesman, April 11, 1876: "John Lemp, director for the First National Bank, is well known to fame as the "Beer King of Idaho," and is one of our wealthier citizens, and at present Mayor of Boise City."

When the Boise City Turnverein Society was established by the Germans of the city at the end of February, 1870, Lemp was elected president. The characteristics of the group, of which he was first choice, were described by *The Statesman* in March, 1870:

"The Germans are peculiarly a musical people, and harmonious not only in the concord of sweet sounds, but in their association with each other. For real genuine sociability, and an old fashioned hearty 'Faderland' re-union and social dancing party, go to the German ball tonight at Slocum's Hall."

Part of Lemp's popularity was due to his sense of humor. After an illness in 1885, which led to considerable fears for his recovery, he was congratulated for his reappearance on Main Street. "I never doubted for a moment that I would recover," he stated. "You see, I had just taken out a new life insurance policy!"

When the city tried out its new chemical fire engine in 1889, the paper reported that "As a wind-up, the crowd went in procession to the residence of Mr. John Lemp on Grove Street, where it is needless to say the amber fluid again fluided until further irrigation would have been a superfluity."

On his 54th birthday, April 21, 1892, the Germania Society and the band surprised John Lemp with a serenade outside his house, singing and playing the old German songs he loved. It was an emotional experience, reflecting the affection and respect Boise City's German-American community felt for the "poor boy who

ISHS 69-81.1

John Lemp (1838-1912) was a classic American success story — a poor immigrant boy who became wealthy in the far West. John and his wife Catherine Kohlepp Lemp raised 13 children.

This lithograph appeared in Elliott's 1884 History of Idaho Territory. Lemp had several saloons in addition to a brewery and this wholesale store.

had made good."

W.A. Goulder, himself an Idaho pioneer, wrote a short reminiscence of his friend Lemp in 1908 entitled "How a Penniless German Boy Made It Go in the Early Days of Idaho." He noted that John Lemp had come to America in 1852, that he had crossed the plains in a wagon train in 1863, and that he had worked as a brewer since he was 14. He did not settle in Boise at once. First he tried his luck in Boise Basin, where most of the mining activity was centered, but two years later he was already listed in the first directory of the area as "proprietor, Boise Brewery."

Civil War Hero

Many of the pioneers of Idaho, and especially of Boise, were natives of Germany. One such was Richard C. Adelmann, and his adventurous early life makes his story a particularly interesting one to recall.

Adelmann was born in Heilbronn, Wurttemburg, on May 8, 1846. He came to America with his parents when eight years of age, at a time when many Germans were leaving the Old World for the new. His mother died only three years later, and the lad was pretty much on his own from then on.

When the Civil War broke out in 1861, young Adelmann was still a schoolboy, but he was so eager to enlist in the Union army that he ran away from home and joined up without his father's knowledge or permission.

He was assigned to the Fifth New York volunteers at Frederick City, Maryland, on August 25, 1862. The outfit was a Zouave unit, which at the start of the war marched into battle in spectacularly exotic costumes in Turkish style: baggy striped pants, embroidered vests, and turbans or fezzes. Richard was a drummer boy with the Zouaves at first, but was soon playing a man's part in some of the bloodiest battles of the war.

Only a month after he enlisted, he was in the three day battle of Antietam, and survived in succession, the harrowing battles of Fredericksburg and Chancellorsville. During the latter fray he was transferred to the 146th New York Infantry, where he soon was promoted to corporal, and with whom he fought at Gettysburg, the Wilderness, and Spottsylvania Courthouse. At North Anna, Virginia, in 1864, he received a serious gunshot wound in the head which affected his vision, and put him in the hospital for several months.

When Confederate General Early made his desperate raid on Washington, D.C., Adelmann again volunteered for active service in defense of the city. When the danger had passed, he again was placed in the hospital, where he spent the rest of the war until his discharge in May, 1865.

He worked in New York City as a confectioner and pastry cook, and then as a grocer for four years before joining his aunt and uncle, Mr. and Mrs. William Jaumann, in the trek to Idaho. They traveled on the new transcontinental railroad as far as Kelton, Utah, and by stagecoach the rest of the way to Boise City, arriving on July 18, 1872.

Richard C. and Julia Ostner Adelmann. She was the daughter of famed pioneer artist Charles Ostner.

ISHS 81-103.1/a,b

The Richard C. Adelmann house at 221 West Jefferson, shortly before its removal to the Pioneer Village in Julia Davis Park, July, 1981.

A dramatic sight indeed was the Adelmann House, being moved along Capitol Boulevard on the morning of July 15, 1981. The Idaho Historical Society saved the century-old building because it was a typical Boise dwelling of earlier days — not because it was a mansion. The homes of average people have historic significance, too.

In Boise, young Adelmann soon became an active member of the community. He was one of the first members of the volunteer fire department when it organized in 1876, and was a volunteer in the Boise City company called together during the Bannock Indian uprising of 1878, serving as Lieutenant.

He was elected fire chief twice, and was also a member of the City Council, the Boise City Turnverein, the Grand Army of the Republic, and the Odd Fellows.

Although a successful Main Street saloon-keeper, Adelmann was a typical Idahoan of his day in that he never gave up the dream of striking it rich in mining. For most of his life he maintained investments in mining properties around the state, and often spent time working the claims himself. He had one such working mine just a few miles above Boise on Cottonwood Creek.

Richard Adelmann was married to Emma Ostner, daughter of famous pioneer-artist Charles Ostner, in 1875. They had two children, Alfred and Carl. After the death of Mrs. Adelmann, he married her sister Julia, with whom he had four more children, William, John, Warren, and Julia.

The Adelmann Building still stands at the northeast corner of Idaho and Capital Boulevard, and Adelmann's modest frame house has been preserved in the Idaho Historical Society's Pioneer Village in Julia Davis Park.

Richard Adelmann loved to parade with other old-timers of Boise's volunteer fire department, with whom he had served so long. Adelmann is the white-bearded man at far right. Park School is in the background.

ISHS 68-23.11

Popular Joe Misseld had a humorous way of expressing himself that got him quoted often in the newspapers. His heavy German accent was easy to imitate, apparently. Joe looks very serious in this studio portrait, but that was not his usual style.

CHARACTERS
Jolly Brewer

 The earliest view we have of Boise's Main Street was painted in 1864 by an artist who signed himself Arm Hincelin. In an ad he later ran in the *Statesman*, Hincelin called himself a "House, Sign, and Ornamental Painter," and offered to do carriage painting, gilding, graining, and paper hanging, "with neatness and dispatch."

He also mentioned portrait and landscape painting, of which the example shown here is the sole known survivor. As interesting as this rare painting is, we should like to concentrate on but one of the business ventures shown in it, and on the colorful Boise pioneer who ran it.

Prominently shown on the right side of the street, just above the covered wagon, is the City Brewery. Its proprietor was a jolly German named Joseph Misseld, and he became one of the community's most popular men. A reason for this was no doubt the obvious one: in a community of miners and adventurers, the brewer supplied a popular commodity. Like his competitor, John Lemp, also from Germany, Joe Misseld knew the value of generosity at the right moments. He could be counted on to tap courtesy-kegs of his brew at public celebrations, political rallies, and for the benefit of the press.

In May, 1871, *The Statesman* bought the adobe building at Sixth and Main, next door to Misseld's City Brewery, and later commented that "The boys think it is a great blessing to have the printing office located in such close proximity to a brewery, especially when the brewer is such a generous soul as Joe Misseld." This was in 1873. The first reference to this happy relationship occurred in August, 1871, shortly after the newspaper moved in next door to the brewery. "Our neighbor, Joe Misseld, remembered this office the other day, and we are now prepared to state, from actual experience, that he makes good lager beer."

In 1872, Misseld made several additions to his brewery, including a large stone ice house. When he filled it the following February, he again celebrated by "filling the printers with lager beer."

The frequency with which the paper printed droll remarks about its popular neighbor suggests other things about him. A "news item" of May, 1876, states simply "Joe Misseld took a drink of water yesterday."

This was followed in the next issue with, "Since Joe Misseld took that drink from Boise River, the water has been falling rapid-

Boise's Early breweries were all run by German-born pioneers. Joe Misseld and John Broadbeck were both associated with the City Brewery, next door to The Statesman *office at 6th and Main.*

ly." The hefty bulk of the thirsty brewer is suggested by this item of 1877: "The reason why Joe Misseld does not go in swimming is because all the water goes out of the pond when he goes in." On the occasion of a race meet in Boise, the boys at *The Statesman* suggested that there was great merit in conducting a "fat man's race," and nominated as their candidate their friend, Joe Misseld. It is noteworthy that in all of the fun poked at the jolly German, a constant note of affection manages to shine through.

One cannot read the pages of the old papers over the years without conceiving one's own affection for some of the pioneers of Idaho, and it must be admitted that we felt a real pang of regret upon reading in the 1879 pages that Joe Misseld had met an untimely end, and in a most unusual way.

Returning to the brewery late one dark night, Misseld fell head-first into his own well and drowned. Because of his size, poor Joe was wedged tightly, and couldn't move to save himself.

*Early Boise saloons looked a lot alike. This is
John Broadbeck's Main Street emporium,
complete with pool tables, kegs of beer, cast iron
stove, bar backed by a mirror, and brass
spittoons. Most served free lunches and snacks.*

Irish Smiles in Boise

 The Irish and their descendents have contributed much to the humor in the pages of Idaho history, giving us anecdotes and witticisms that have been repeated with relish for over a century.

Many of the immigrants driven from the Emerald Isle in the Nineteenth Century by hard times and famine eventually found themselves in the mountains of the west seeking their fortunes in the gold camps. Some came west as recruits in the army, other employment being hard to find. For whatever reason they came, and under whatever difficult conditions they labored, their native gift of humor and fancy came out, cheering the way for their fellow pioneers.

Jimmy Hart, a jovial saloonkeeper of Boise, was typical. He had been in California during the gold fever there and had drifted north to Idaho in October of 1861, with thousands of others hoping to strike it rich in the North Idaho mines. After a time in Orofino and Florence, working mostly as a bartender, Hart went with the crowds into Boise Basin. He owned and operated Jim's Drinking Saloon at Placerville before moving to Boise and going to work for Johnny Crowe, another pioneer saloon man, formerly of Idaho City.

Hart's Irish wit was soon turned to good advantage by his employer, who started sending Jimmy's latest pronouncements to *The Statesman* . They were, in effect, the paper's humor column; they were also fine advertising for Johnny Crowe's "Sample Rooms," as saloons were called at the time. There are indications that Crowe kept a good thing going by sending frequent liquid encouragement to the *Statesman* office — a common example of the barter system then in use.

In the mid-Seventies, Crowe sold out to his popular employee, and Jimmy's news items became a feature of just about every issue of the paper for twenty years. "The indigent, sick, idiotic and insane will be fed with Clam chowder at Jimmy Hart's tonight, as the hospital is undergoing a frescoing," he wrote in 1882, tying his comment to a current local event.

When the weather got cold, he commented, "As water freezes now every night, Jimmy Hart thinks it is his duty to warn his friends not to take too freely of that kind of fluid, or they will wake up some morning with a skating pond in their stomachs."

Clam chowder was Jimmy Hart's specialty, the clams coming

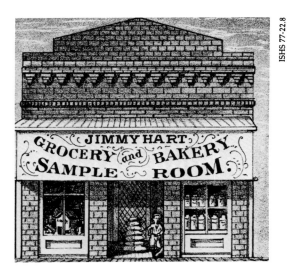

Jimmy Hart's establishment looked like this in 1878, according to Charles Ostner's lithographic view. "Sample Room" was another name for saloon.

by wagon from Puget Sound. When the weather was too hot for this, even with a packing of ice, he switched to pork and beans or baked ham — both plentiful locally.

On July 1, 1876, Jimmy announced his special treat for the national centennial celebration. ". . . baked beans — free for all. All kinds of fancy iced drinks, not free!." After being defeated in a local election, he wrote, "Jimmy Hart won't dish up more than 77 plates of clam chowder hereafter — a merited punishment to all who voted against him." (He had received just 77 votes.)

When Boise's new fire department paraded for the nation's hundredth birthday on July 4, 1876, it was noted that "Jimmy Hart will be chief fireman today, and will ride the Hook and Ladder Truck." He was an active member of the company for many years.

When the legislature was in session, Democrat Hart had fun wording his quips to attract Republicans to his saloon, such as announcing that a "solid Democratic ham will be cut up for the Republican legislators this Saturday night." He later said that his chowder would be "red hot for the benefit of the Idaho Parliament who do not like to gulp things down without referring to a committee," and called his rye whiskey "the best electioneering documents to be found." He invited his patrons to "vote every day as often as you please."

In a rueful reference to his shortcomings as a farmer, Hart once said that he had harvested his strawberry crop, and had "picked enough ripe strawberries to give each of his children one."

Diamond-tooth Lil

 The shady lady with a heart of gold is a stock character in stories about the Old West. Boise had such a real life character, more famous for a tooth of gold than for her heart, although that was probably fourteen carat, too.

"Diamond-tooth Lil" was her name, and like many another character in Western lore, she devoted a lifetime to perfecting her own legend and image. Lil not only had a prominent gold tooth in the middle of her smile, but a large diamond was set in the middle of it. This made her stand out in any company, and that's the way Lil loved it, for ever since childhood she had hungered for recognition and thirsted for fame.

All of the facts we have about Lil's colorful life come from her own reminiscences, recounted through the years to just about any reporter who would listen. Whether her stories were true never seemed too important, since they made such good telling.

Mae West's movie characterization of "Diamond Lil" was based on Lil's life, and she has found her way into a number of recent books on the Old West. One striking similarity in all the accounts we have read is the stress laid on Diamond-tooth Lil's beauty and glamor. Words like "fabulous" and "exciting" are regularly used to describe her, although the photographs at the Idaho Historical Society hardly bear this out. Perhaps it was Lil's undoubted vitality and sense of showmanship that created the illusion. At least one local man who knew her says she was "quite plain, really." Another says she was "plump and dowdy," but in fairness, these men never saw her in her prime. The photographs we have show Lil as a girl, and as she looked in later life when she lived in Boise. Our readers may draw their own conclusions.

We shall content ourselves with telling the rest of her story as she herself often told it:

Evelyn Hildegarde was born Katie Prado near Vienna, Austria, about 1880. Many of the facts in the various interviews she gave don't match up exactly, but it appears that she and her parents came to America when she was six, that her father was Austrian and her mother Bohemian, and that she ran away from home when she was thirteen. She eloped with 19-year-old Percy Hildegarde, and used his name the rest of her life, although by her own account, she had a total of eight other husbands. Lil apparently never worried about ridding herself of any previous husband, she

The Depot Inn, operated for many years by "Diamond-tooth Lil" Hildegarde, was more than a motel. This post card view was made in 1933.

ISHS 69-146.1/a

ISHS 69-146.1/c

ISHS 63.204

This series of portraits shows Evelyn Hildegard from 1918 until 1963. She herself signed the earliest of them "Diamond Lil," after Mae West's movie of that name, claiming that it was her story.

just took another when the mood struck her.

Among the men in her life, not all of whom made it legal, were some pretty colorful characters in their own right: Prizefighter Kid McCoy, Spider Kelly, Diamondfield Jack Davis, Tex Rickard and Tom Sharkey.

Diamond-tooth Lil's friendship with Diamondfield Jack was a natural. The swaggering Jack had enough color of his own to fill several books, and although notorious as a gunman, his chief claim to fame in Idaho is that he was almost hung for a murder he didn't commit. Jack may have been the inspiration for Lil's famous dental job. They met in 1907 in the boomtown of Goldfield, Nevada, after Lil had already been singing and dancing in music halls and gambling palaces for several years. After a shooting scrape in Goldfield, Jack took off for New York and Lil went with him. Many years later, when they were both past 70, they had a reunion in Las Vegas, much publicized at the time.

Lil claims she was the "toast of the Barbary Coast" in San Francisco, and a star at the St. Louis World's Fair of 1904. Somewhere along the way, she got in on the gold rush to Alaska, and came to Silver City, Idaho, after that. Boise was her home from 1909 until 1943, during which time she ran rooming houses and opened the Depot Inn in 1933.

Diamond-tooth Lil's experience as a "business-woman" extended far back before that. She says she was in business from the time she was thirteen, and ran large houses in Chicago, St. Louis, New York and Seattle. One of her "bosses" in Chicago was Al Capone, and it is no surprise that her memories of the gangster era include some pretty grim incidents of killings and violence. She herself was shot at by an ex-husband in El Paso, Texas.

Charitable and generous, Lil felt a special sympathy for orphans, and when she left Boise, had promised to will her famous tooth (now set in her dentures) to the Boise Children's Home. However, she died in California at 89, and the tooth that made her famous was buried with her.

Demolition of the Levy's Alley area by Urban Renewal to make way for Boise's new City Hall marked the end of the center of "flaming vice" in the neighborhood. The "Lodging House" in this photo is one of those shown on the 1903 fire map. Photo by author, January 6, 1975.

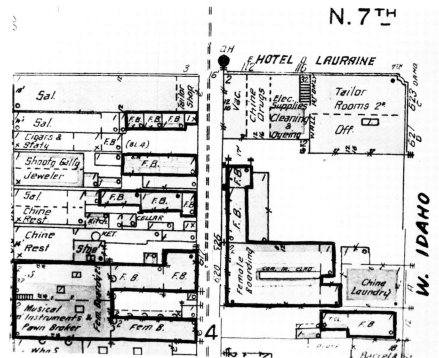

Notorious Levy's Alley, in the block bounded by Sixth and Seventh, Main and Idaho, was largely made up of "Female Boarding" houses, as this 1903 fire map shows (sometimes abbreviated to "F.B."). Anti-vice crusades from the late 1880s until this time had failed to dislodge Boise's red light district from its traditional location.

Hogan the Stiff

Occasionally an obscure figure in local history intrigues the researcher. Such a person was "Hogan the Stiff," known to just about everyone in Boise at the turn of the century.

We first got interested in Hogan when we ran across the picture shown here, taken in the Ada County Sheriff's office in 1901. It shows Sheriff Joe Daly, his wife and two daughters, a lady clerk, Deputy Andy Robinson, and rather pathetically, the small figure of a man in irons, labeled simply, "Hogan the Stiff."

Our first reaction was that the sheriff had done a rather strange thing in having his wife and little girls pose with a prisoner. Was Hogan a dangerous killer? A burglar? He looks rather harmless to be locked in irons, and the sheriff looks big enough to handle him without them. The nickname "the Stiff" suggested anything from ghoulish grave robber to town drunk, but our picture label contained no further information about Hogan.

Months later came our first clue to the true identity of Hogan. While scanning old newspapers in search of something else, we

"Hogan the Stiff" is the sad little man in irons in this 1901 photo made in the office of Ada County Sheriff Joe Daly. Mrs. Daly and daughters are at left. The Sheriff has an arm around his most regular customer, and Deputy Andy Robinson is at right. The woman at the desk is the office clerk.

ISHS 1957

ran across an account of the arrest of "Hogan the Stiff," who was "again in jail for vagrancy." The reporter, writing in May, 1894, noted that "It is a three months' dose this time," suggesting that this was nothing new.

In the course of subsequent research, and in conversations with a number of old-time Boiseans, we have compiled quite a dossier on Hogan. While not without a certain humor, the misadventures of this man suggest all too clearly the pathetic and even tragic life of an alcoholic. They also point out that nobody knew how to help him, even though he was generally regarded with tolerance and treated kindly.

Ten years after the jailing reported above, Hogan was the subject of a news story in which he made a plea to be called "just plain Jimmy." He told the reporter he didn't like the stories written about him (and by 1904 there had been a great many). These stories usually treated Hogan's misfortunes in a humorous vein, regarding him as a town character.

On one occasion in 1907, Hogan was passing a music store with a phonograph playing outside. The record was one with a "laughing song" on it, and the sidewalk listeners were laughing, too. Thinking they were laughing at him, Hogan got a brick and smashed the machine. "Thirty days," said the judge.

Harry Shellworth of Boise, whose father was chief of police during part of Hogan's era, recalled seeing the unfortunate in handcuffs on Main Street. As he was led along by a policeman, he sang, rather sadly, to the tune of "The Bear Went Over the Mountain," "I'm on my way to the jail house, and nobody gives a damn!"

Shellworth also suggested the reason for the handcuffs and leg irons in our photograph by recalling that Boise's first padded cell was installed in the city jail to keep Hogan from injuring himself during his attacks of delirium tremens. For many years he was a regular "boarder" in the jail, often timing his arrests to secure winter quarters.

Architect Fritz Hummel recalled that Hogan did farm work for John Lemp, and that he went on a "bender" whenever he came to town. Lemp apparently bailed him out and tried to keep him on the ranch.

Attorney James H. Hawley especially remembered a day when "Hogan the Stiff" met one of Boise's most elegant and fashionable ladies, Mrs. Alfred Eoff, crossing Main Street on a narrow path through the mud. Hogan stepped off into the deep mud and removed his hat. Mrs. Eoff said, "It's a muddy day, Mr. Hogan." "It's a damned muddy day, Mrs. Eoff," replied Hogan, standing ankle deep to let her pass.

James Hogan was a native of Tipperary, Ireland, born March 12, 1834. He arrived in America in 1848, and started to California to look for gold in 1853, arriving in January, 1854. He came to Idaho in 1863, going first to Placerville, and then to Boise where he went to work as a cook in the Overland Hotel. He was still listed as a cook in the Boise City directories of 1899 and 1901.

WHEELS THROUGH BOISE

By 1887, when this engraving was published, Boise City had a Main Street lined with substantial buildings of brick and stone. Covered wagons were still prominent. Overland Hotel is on the right, Richard Adelmann's Gem Saloon, far left, and Frank Coffin's tin shop, marked by a big tin coffee pot sign, is near center.

The Endless Procession

The streets of Boise City in 1881 were filled with colorful sights and sounds that many of us would enjoy experiencing for ourselves, were it only possible to break the time barrier and return for a short visit to the little town of over a century ago. Through the pages of our old newspapers, however, we can still recapture much of what Boiseans saw, heard and were concerned about.

Probably we would be most impressed by the compactness of the little city, and the small scale of its buildings. John Lemp was putting up the first three-story building the city had seen, and a number of other new brick stores were being erected to replace wooden ones lost in a recent fire on Main Street.

The streets themselves were crowded with people and wagons most of the time. Many were emigrant "prairie schooners" following the Oregon Trail, and 1881 saw so many of them that *The Statesman* made frequent observations like this one: "The Endless Procession. — All day long we see the steady caravan of canvas-topped wagons passing through Main Street or halting in front of some store door to replenish the stock of corn meal and bacon."

An average of twenty wagons a day passed through the city that summer, many of them bound for the Palouse and places other than western Oregon, which had been the goal of most of the emigrants of earlier days. One wagon had a sign on it that read:

"I bid Kansas farewell;
Never mind what I may do,
I may emigrate to hell,
But never back to you."

Others carried the old favorite, "Oregon or Bust."

Many Idaho localities received new population via the trail (and Boise's Main Street) that summer, including the Weiser and Payette river valleys, and by October the few stragglers coming through were faced with the prospect of an Idaho winter camp, whether they had planned on it or not. Early snows could make further progress impossible or foolhardy. Always wishing to attract new population and business for local merchants, *The Statesman* ominously predicted that "most of them that have gone to the Columbia Valley will wish they had stayed here, before the spring comes around."

In a classic description of these emigrants passing through, a *Statesman* reporter penned this in October, 1881: "The old gray horses, the old man with the grizzly beard, the stout old woman sitting on the rawhide chair with the corncob pipe, and last but not least, the old brown dog under the rickety wagon, all these familiar pictures have vanished from our sight for the year. Next year like pictures will be seen on our streets, as the great army for free labor moves westward in its march of progress. A few weeks more and the stages will be our only vehicles."

Although no photographer captured the vivid scene described above, there is an engraving in William Thayer's *Marvels of the New West* that shows Boise's Main Street in the Eighties with covered wagons, small buildings, and the compact look of the neat little town on the old Oregon Trail.

Covered wagons were a familiar sight on Boise's Main Street from 1863 until well into the Twentieth Century. This 1866 photo captures in a classic way the hustle and bustle of a frontier town.

ISHS 73

"Uncle John" Hailey was placed in charge of the Idaho State Historical Society in 1907 when the legislature made it a state agency. He began the collections that became the State Museum.

Stagecoach King

 When the old man died they placed his casket under the dome of Idaho's Capitol and closed all the state offices. Downtown Boise businesses also closed on the day of the funeral of Idaho's great stagecoach king, "Uncle John" Hailey.

John Hailey not only operated more than 2,000 miles of stage lines in Washington, Oregon, California, Idaho, Montana, Nevada and Utah, but was also a leader in other pioneer enterprises in the Pacific Northwest. He operated early saddle trains into Idaho's gold camps, founded the city of Hailey, and operated a gold mine south of Bellevue. A pioneer sheep raiser, he turned to stock raising and farming as rail lines replaced stages. As a famous early settler, he was a leading member of the Historical Society of Idaho Pioneers, founded in 1881, and when this organization became the Idaho State Historical Society, by act of the legislature in 1907, John Hailey was named its first curator and librarian. He also, at the request of the legislature, wrote a history of Idaho published in 1910.

For most of his life he was called "the Honorable John Hailey," for he had served as delegate to Congress from Idaho Territory in 1873-75, and again in 1885-87. He was elected to the Territorial Legislature also, and was chosen Council President in 1880-81. During his campaigns for office he was often called "honest John." In 1889 he was appointed warden of the penitentiary. He was elected mayor of Boise in 1871, but apparently did not serve, perhaps because of the Congressional race just ahead.

The prelude to Hailey's Idaho accomplishments is equally colorful and noteworthy. As a boy of 17 he crossed the plains to Oregon in a wagon train. Hostile Indians attacked the emigrants twice along the way, driving off the horses and making it necessary to drive the cattle on foot the rest of the way. In Oregon his first job was as an axeman, his second was as a miner, and his third was as a volunteer Indian fighter in the 1855-56 uprising at Rogue River. Many years later Hailey still had his canteen and ammunition belt from that experience, and placed them in the State Historical Museum which he was working to expand.

The sight of an old Idaho stagecoach in a Boise parade in 1907 drew forth the following reminiscence from "Uncle John":

"When I saw that old stage in the parade, decorated with sagebrush, and being drawn by mismated horses, I felt like turning

*John Hailey and some of the stagecoach drivers
who had worked for him in earlier days posed for
this picture in about 1910.*

my head and not looking at it — such a burlesque. That looked nothing like the old-time stagecoaches. They should have had six spirited horses and the coach stacked with trunks and baggage in the rear and on top, and a dozen or so persons riding, then they would have had a coach similar to the ones we used to drive. I've carried as many as 24 persons at a time, many of them riding on top of the coach. People used to sit at the Overland Hotel until 2 o'clock in the morning just to see the stage start out. The driver used to come down the street at a clanking trot, and the horses were trained so they would whirl in at the hotel with a flourish. They were always pulling against the bit and ready to go."

Idaho's stagecoach king is shown with a group of his pioneer drivers in a reunion picture taken in the early years of the 20th Century. Hailey is seated at the right on the driver's seat of a "mud wagon" like the one in the Idaho Historical Museum.

"Uncle John" made and lost several fortunes in his life, but he never lost his love of Idaho history, or the respect and affection of those who thought him its living embodiment.

John and Louisa Griffith Hailey, at about the time he was elected to a second term in Congress representing Idaho Territory. He was already renowned as a stagecoach and sheep king. The Haileys raised six children.

ISHS 81-68.2,3

Bicycle Mania

 The bicycle craze hit Idaho in the late 1880s. By 1892, the new form of transportation was tremendously popular in towns and cities, not only for recreation, but for going to and from school and work.

Forerunners of the bicycle were seen in Boise as early as 1869, and were known as velocipedes. In those days, quite a variety of contraptions were called by this name, but most were like that ridden by Ben Larkin, referred to in an *Idaho Tri-weekly Statesman* story on April 3, 1869, as a "two-wheeled red waggin."

The story was headed "Velocipede Mania," and referred to Larkin's bicycle riding in some amusement, although the unfamiliar word was spelled "bycicle." Larkin's machine was imported from San Francisco, but two Boise blacksmiths built their own, described by the reporter as an "improved design." He also noted that "the velocipede mania, which at one time seemed to be dying out, is now on the increase decidedly."

This early craze did pass rather quickly, however, probably because Idaho roads and streets were just too rough for two-wheeled vehicles with wooden wheels and no springs. Other early accounts sometimes referred to the first bikes as "bone-shakers," a term that must have been accurately descriptive.

An engraving of Idaho's Territorial Capitol Building, published in 1887, shows Capitol Square; the buildings, left to right, are Central School, the Capitol, and the Ada County Courthouse. (The present Capitol now occupies the space.)

Especially interesting are the two high-wheel bicycle riders in the foreground. Their presence in this bustling scene suggests that the high-wheelers were common by this time. One such machine has survived and is on display in the Idaho Historical Society's Transportation Museum at the Old Penitentiary.

ISHS 80-149.1

This bicycling couple are Mr. and Mrs. Manlove Hull. Pride in their shiny new machines must have prompted this studio portrait. Mr. Hull's head lamp is much like that used by underground miners.

Muddy streets did not discourage avid cyclists. When many of them began riding on the sidewalks, the city banned it as hazardous to pedestrians. Sonna's Opera House at Ninth and Main is in the background, with a heavy freight team ready to pull out for the mines.

ISHS 1951

A photograph taken in the late 1890s shows a group of Boiseans in front of a house at Tenth and Hays Streets. Three bicycles add interest to this scene as does the distinguished gent at far right. He is John M. Haines, mayor, and Governor of Idaho from 1912 until 1914. When this picture was taken, Haines was active in the firm of W.E. Pierce and Co., real estate developers. These bicycles, too, are similar to ones in the museum collection. Pneumatic tires have replaced the old hard rubber ones of a few years earlier, although some bicycles still had wooden handlebars and fenders.

On June 15, 1892, the Capital City Cycling Club was formed at the Y.M.C.A. Officers were elected, and activities planned. The first road tour undertaken by the group was an ambitious one — they rode to Nampa for the night, got up at 4 a.m., rode to Walters Ferry for lunch, and continued on to Silver City the same day. Since bicycles of that time did not have gear shifts, part of that June day in 1892 was spent pushing. Club members proudly claimed a 45 mile trip that day, but they must have walked at least ten of it.

In July, the cyclists were racing on Seventh Street. The local record set at that time was 300 yards in 39 seconds, and readers of Idaho papers began to take special interest in reports from the East of record times made by famous "wheelmen" in races there. *The Statesman* now regularly published pictures of this new kind of American athletic hero, as the bicycle craze swept across the country. Each big Eastern racing meet was reported in as much detail as baseball or football contests, as the nation experienced the first of several revivals of interest in bicycling.

Bicycles were "the thing" when this late 1890s picture was taken. Note the cast iron hitching post, center. John M. Haines, far right, would later be elected mayor of Boise and governor of Idaho.

Telegrams were hand-delivered by messenger boys on bicycles from the 1890s until after World War II. (Some of the "boys" were actually elderly men).

This unidentified Boise Chinese man liked cycling enough to have a studio portrait made with his bike, trouser clipped right ankle and a buttonhole rose.

Rapid Transit

 The removal in recent years of some old street railway tracks, buried for decades under Boise's downtown asphalt, recalled for many an era in transportation long gone in Idaho.

Boise's first streetcar operation was chartered on May 28, 1890. This firm, the Boise Rapid Transit Company, started building a little over a year later, just about the time plans for the Natatorium two miles east of town on Warm Springs Avenue were being completed.

By the Fourth of July, 1891, the tracks were completed to the Natatorium site. In August, the cars were ready for testing: . . . "the street was crowded with spectators eager to see how the new-fangled arrangement would work. Car No. 2 was run up Main Street for quite a distance, though slowly and cautiously."

At the end of August, Boiseans were getting up "rapid transit parties," and enjoying the novelty of riding streetcars for the first time. It was reported at the start of September that at least 1,500 people were riding each day. Two days later this estimate was reduced to 800 — still an impressive figure for a town of about 4,000 people.

Each tiny car had a motorman and a conductor, but they didn't always see eye to eye on the operation of their machine. It may have been a hot dusty day, or it may have been an accumulation of annoyances, but in July, 1892, Motorman Ed Moore and Conductor Lane "quarreled about the running of the car, and as soon as they reached a convenient spot, they went at it hammer and tongs. Moore is the larger man, but Lane quickly picked up a stone, and as David did Goliath, he smote Moore with great vigor."

Summer streetcar riding is a joy unknown to the present generation, but it was tremendously popular in Boise Valley for 30 years. The Rapid Transit Company bought its first open cars for use in the summer of 1892. In 1904 the new larger cars added to the system were "half open and half closed." The Interurban line, which began operation in 1907, also used open cars on its loop down the valley to Middleton and Caldwell. Many an old-timer wistfully recalls the delight of humming along the rails in an open car on a summer's day.

The machines were remarkably quiet and clean, compared to the buses we have now, and the rails provided a smoother ride

By 1920, when this Boise Valley Traction Company car was photographed, the Interurban line to Caldwell and back had been operating for a dozen years. There were a series of small stations like this one where freight and passengers could be picked up.

Eighth and Main was Boise's chief intersection when photographer R.H. Sigler took this 1915 view. The streetcar at left has little traffic to contend with, but the automobiles now in evidence would soon kill the street railway business.

than many streets and roads do today. Part of the special pleasure of the Interurban came from the fact that there was little traffic to worry about, and that most of the ride through the Boise Valley was in open countryside.

Families could take a picnic lunch, have a pleasant ride through the virgin sagebrush or lush irrigated farmlands along the tracks, and stop at one of the parks maintained by the company for just such occasions. Curtis Park on the north side of Boise River between Caldwell and Middleton, was one such picnic place. Pierce Park, where Plantation Golf Course is today, was another.

Before automobiles took over, electric street railways were able to provide fast, safe, and economical transportation for everyone. As more and more people bought cars, the volume of streetcar business declined, forcing fares upward. Costs of maintaining tracks and facilities increased at the same time patronage was declining, eventually forcing this efficient form of public transportation out of business. Boise's last streetcar trip ended at 12:30 a.m., June 15, 1927.

Our two photographs illustrate part of the charm of life in Boise's streetcar era. Open car No. 45 stars in both scenes — first in July, 1906, near 17th and Irene Streets, and in about 1915 at the corner of Eight and Main. Aside from pedestrians, only two bicycles made up downtown traffic the morning the picture was snapped. The two cars on Eighth had parking competition from only three bicycles.

Street cars began service to new north end neighborhoods in the mid-Nineties, and were a significant factor in the growth of the city wherever the lines run. Commuters could leave the horses at home and ride to work for a modest fare.

Open cars, like Boise Rapid Transit #45, were appreciated in summer. This July, 1906 photo shows Hubert Shaw and Fred Bennett, and advertising for an opera performance at Riverside Park.

Boise Rapid Transit Company's car number one began running in August, 1891. These first trolleys were so small that when one jumped the tracks the passengers got off and lifted it back.

Main Street, looking west from the corner of Sixth, looked like this in about 1900. The streetcar is headed for Warm Springs Avenue and the Natatorium.

Touring Cars

Tourism did not significantly affect Boise's economy until the automobile became common. Railroads had contributed to the development of scenic locations, natural hot springs and resorts, but large scale recreational travel did not occur until most families had cars of their own.

Boiseans began taking their autos into the back country very early, despite an almost total lack of improved roads. There were no paved roads at all, and only a few streets in larger cities were hard surfaced. Boise's Main Street was not paved until 1897 — with wooden blocks set in sand and asphalt — but there were not yet any automobiles in town.

By 1907 Boise had the "auto craze," as *The Idaho Statesman* put it, and an auto club was formed. That year the first car from the valley chugged into Silver City, and other mountain towns soon saw their first gas buggies as well. In 1909 intrepid Nevada tourists braved the desert to drive from Winnemucca to Caldwell. The 270 mile trip took 48 hours.

By the 1920s automobiles were so numerous that Idaho cities and towns were having trouble finding places to park them. Nampa established a tourist park for visiting motorists in 1923 that registered 523 cars that season. (258 of them were Ford Model Ts). Twin Falls opened a tourist park in 1924 that was used by the astonishing number of 2700 vehicles in its first summer.

"Motor Camping Grows Yearly" said *The Statesman* in 1926, noting that there was now a "chain of tourist camps" across the state. "A few years ago the man who packed his wife and children into the family car and started out for an automobile camping trip was almost subject to arrest for cruelty, but this year the motorists who choose this form of vacation will do it in style."

This new mobility made Idaho aware that it had unique assets that could attract out-of-state travelers, and that if they came, they would spend a significant amount of money here. Shoshone Falls had achieved national fame early and had been promoted by the Union Pacific, along with Soda Springs and Hailey Hot Springs, but there was a new awareness that the state had much more to offer.

Nobody was more active in preaching the benefits of developing tourism in Idaho than Boise taxidermist Robert Limbert. He was a pioneer in urging the creation of a National Park at what

ISHS 62-19.1136

Hill climbing tests were popular in the early days of motoring. Rupert Shaw captured this action on "Slaughterhouse Hill" near the present Highlands, in about 1920. The car is an Oldsmobile.

Tourist camps had been set up in most Idaho towns by the 1920s. This one was in Boise among cottonwood trees beside the river.

Rupert Shaw's family made an early run to Silver City in their 1912 Winton. Young Rupert recorded the arrival in front of the old town's Idaho Hotel.

eventually became Craters of the Moon National Monument. In November, 1923, he showed stereopticon slides of the dramatic area to the Boise Chamber of Commerce, and urged the group to work toward the development of a tourist park and pack trails there. Largely as a result of his efforts, a Craters of the Moon National Park Association was formed that year, with Mayor E.W. Schubert of Pocatello as president.

Another early advocate of Craters of the Moon as a tourist attraction was S.O. Paisley of Arco. He was named "custodian" of the Craters in 1925, at an annual salary of $12. This gave him the distinction, he said, of being the lowest paid person on the federal payroll.

Robert Limbert, who lectured widely on nature subjects in the 1920s, was instrumental in bringing the Seattle Mountaineers and the Mount Stuart Alpine Club to Craters of the Moon in 1926. He continued to urge Idahoans to realize that tourism was important to the state's future.

Family outings into the sagebrush or the mountains were a feature of early automobiling. They still are. This 1912 Winton contrasts interestingly with a donkey cart.

Henry Alegria, Basque pioneer, was an enthusiastic motorist. On September 5, 1920, he drove this Overland four cylinder touring car over an 18 foot gap between ramps at Boise Barracks.

These early Boise autos are parked in front of the Bell Telephone building near Sixth and Main. The motorcycle at left reminds us that the two-wheelers became popular at the same time.

Not a single automobile can be seen in this turn-of-the-century view of Main Street at the corner of Tenth. Probably the street had been cleared for a holiday parade.

Believe it or not, Boise once had a Ford Assembly plant, operated by H.H. Bryant, Henry Ford's brother-in-law. These "black beauties" with shining brass fittings were lined up against a small-town background very unlike Detroit.

DAYS TO REMEMBER

ISHS 76-114.8/e

The Ladies of the Grand Army of the Republic dedicated this statue of Abraham Lincoln on the grounds of the Idaho Soldiers Home in July, 1915. They were wives and daughters of Union veterans of the Civil War.

Remembering Lincoln

 Pictures of Abraham Lincoln once hung in just about every schoolroom in Idaho. At the tree-shaded grounds of the Idaho Soldiers Home on State Street, now Veteran's Memorial Park, the Ladies of the Grand Army of the Republic in 1915 presented the state with a handsome bronze statue of the martyred president, to commemorate his birthday.

In view of the almost universal reverence for Lincoln's memory today, it is enlightening to recall the mixed reaction in Idaho when news of his assassination reached this isolated frontier territory.

"Last Thursday was the saddest day ever seen in Boise City," wrote the Republican editor of *The Statesman* on April 29, 1865. "The frightful news had shocked the people so that they stood aghast with terror the day before; but then, recovering partially upon the doubt that the first report was true, men tried to assume an air of some cheerfulness. But confirmation came at last, and the stoutest heart gave way . . .".

It had taken more than two weeks for the news to reach Idaho. In most towns, as in Boise City, "business by common consent was entirely closed and the whole city set in mourning. Stiller and more solemn than any Sabbath day in a New England hamlet. No sound or stir of business, people appeared as if each had lost a member of his household."

One by one the reports came in from other Idaho communities. Not too surprisingly, considering the number of Southerners in the mining areas, the reaction was not all one of sorrow. From Ruby City came the report that "there were several unprincipled and ignorant persons who expressed gratification at the intelligence, thus staining themselves with treason for all time to come. They are not worth notice, or I would report them," continued the correspondent. He had apparently seen an order from Army headquarters in San Francisco, circulated throughout the West, which read: "It has come to the knowledge of the Major General Commanding, that there have been found within the Department, persons so utterly infamous as to exult over the assassination of the President. Such persons become virtually accessories after the fact, and will at once be arrested by the provost marshal, any officer or member of the police having knowledge of the case.

Any paper so offending, or expressing any sympathy in any way whatever, will be at once seized and suppressed."

This warning to newspapers obviously did not daunt the pro-Southern *Idaho World* at Idaho City. In a dialect story, intended to be funny, the *World* said that "Ole Dabe . . . is in Dixie Land. He was playin a tragedy in a theater, and played it too natteral. He succeeded better in comedy or a joke . . ." The Republican *Idaho Statesman* was furious at this unpunished infamy, and called it "fiendish."

The citizens of Pioneer City, another Boise Basin mining camp with many Southerners, also showed a mixed reaction to the news. "Some certain individuals seemed to be well pleased to hear of the President's death," wrote a correspondent, "while others shed many sorrowful tears over it."

There were other reports noting the revenge that communities had taken against those so brash as to exult in presidential assassination. One miner in Nevada, known as "Barley Jake," was run out of the country. He escaped with his life, but had to abandon $7,000 worth of property, a source of obvious satisfaction to the paper that reported it.

Idaho's best-known statue of Abraham Lincoln still stands, at its second location in front of the present Idaho Soldiers Home adjoining the grounds of old Fort Boise. The fort was established July 3, 1863, while Lincoln was president and while the battle of Gettysburg was being fought, making this an appropriate site for his monument.

Departure of the Volunteers

When America went to war against Spain in 1898 a fever of patriotism gripped the country. Cuba's struggle for independence had secured the sympathy of most Boiseans and propaganda in American newspapers accusing the Spaniards of every kind of atrocity had stirred people into a desire to punish them.

Even Mexican pioneer Jesus Urquidez, one of the city's earliest settlers, was attacked as a "Spaniard" because he spoke that language. Historians now regard American participation in the war with Spain as in large measure due to a "yellow journalism" that did all it could to make the country fighting mad by distorted appeals to emotion.

There were also those who saw the events in Cuba as an opportunity for America to become a colonial power at small cost, for the Spanish empire was too large and scattered to be defended against a much richer and more powerful America with an expanding and modern navy.

Boise experienced a fever of patriotism on May 19, 1898, when Idaho troops marched to the railroad station on Front Street to depart for the war. The newspaper headline that day said they were off "to join Dewey," for news of Admiral Dewey's defeat of the Spanish fleet at Manila Bay in the far-off Philippines had recently arrived.

Snapshots of that memorable day in the city's history were discovered in an album in a San Francisco trunk in 1972. They were then acquired by the Idaho Historical Society. A Boise volunteer fireman, Charles H. Beck, had taken the pictures and prepared the album for a friend. They are a vivid record of Boise's mood on that historic occasion.

Since the fire department took part in the capital city's big send-off for the soldiers, there is a photo of the firemen drawn up on Fourth Street facing Jefferson as the "boys in blue" march past. They were scheduled to fall into line in the parade as soon as the mayor and city council had joined it ahead of them. These city officials can be seen in the right side of the photo in two open carriages bedecked with flags. Moses Alexander was mayor at the time, and had issued a special proclamation two days before urging Boiseans "to decorate their residences and places of business, particularly along the line of march, for this occasion."

A second memorable glimpse of that day in May is afforded by

Respected pioneer packer Jesus Urquidez was bullied during the Spanish-American War because he was perceived as a Spaniard. Actually, he was Mexican of Basque descent.

These snapshots recall the excitement of the departure of Idaho volunteers and regulars for the Spanish-American War of 1898.

a photograph in the album which shows the excitement and enthusiasm of the crowd. As the soldiers swing past, packs on their backs and rifles on their shoulders, several small boys trot delightedly along beside them, never taking their eyes off their heroes. All of the boys are dressed up for the occasion, and all wear hats or caps. At least two of them wear "Lord Fauntleroy" jackets with white collars. Two excited young women are also hurrying along in this fine action picture, dressed in the elegant fashions of the Nineties.

The Boise we can see in the background of these pictures is a youthful city of dirt streets, small trees and neat cottages.

Drama at the Courthouse

The bombing assassination of former Governor Frank Steunenberg on December 30, 1905, focused national attention on Idaho, and the sensational trial of "Big Bill" Haywood, following the capture of Harry Orchard, the confessed assassin, created even more of a stir in 1907.

A number of men were brought into national prominence as a result of the case, and the names of some are still household words in Idaho.

The lasting fame of Steunenberg, whose statue faces the Idaho Capitol, was due largely to the martyrdom he suffered for his actions in attempting to restore law and order to the strife-ridden Coeur d'Alene mining region. There had been trouble there between labor and management since 1892, and in 1899 the blowing up of the Bunker Hill and Sullivan concentrator led the governor to proclaim martial law, and call in the troops. Union miners considered this to be part of a conspiracy between government and owners to coerce the workers, since the leaders of organized labor had already been loudly proclaiming such a conspiracy for some time across the nation.

The horror of the dynamite blast that killed Steunenberg, as he opened his garden gate in Caldwell, was followed by even more shock to the public when the confession of the dynamiter, Orchard, was published. Not only did Harry Orchard tell in detail how he planted the explosive charge that killed the former governor, he blithely confessed to more than twenty other similar crimes against enemies of the Western Federation of Miners, claiming that he had been hired by the union to commit them, and paid out of its treasury.

Before the confession was released to the newspapers, the State of Idaho had worked some intricate secret maneuvers to get three union leaders in Colorado extradited to Boise for trial as conspirators. After the three were spirited to Idaho by special train, more than a year of court action over the legality of the extradition delayed the trial, ending finally in a decision by the Supreme Court of the United States upholding the action.

Most famous of the Western Federation leaders was William "Big Bill" Haywood. After a trial marked by brilliant handling on both sides, in which Orchard was star witness for the prosecution, Haywood's noted attorney Clarence Darrow secured an

Harry Orchard, alias Thomas Hogan, looked like this shortly after his capture in January, 1906.

This was the scene in Ada County Courthouse on June 13, 1907. Harry Orchard is on the witness stand, left. Clarence Darrow, the famed defense attorney, is labeled #9, right of center, and William Haywood is #11 at right. Darrow secured an acquittal for Haywood.

When he appeared as star witness for the prosecution in the trial of Big Bill Haywood in 1907, Harry Orchard had grown a moustache and sported a new suit of clothes.

These 1909 "mug shots" of Orchard were taken at the Idaho Penitentiary. He would spend the rest of his life there.

acquittal. Darrow, of course, went on to fame as perhaps America's greatest defense attorney. William E. Borah and James H. Hawley, the prosecutors, also came out of the case with enhanced reputations, in spite of Haywood's acquittal, and went on to successful political careers.

Orchard lived out his life in the Idaho Penitentiary, after a religious conversion which won him wide sympathy, even with some members of the Steunenberg family.

Haywood continued to be one of the most controversial radical leaders of the century after his acquittal. He had earlier founded the Industrial Workers of the World, or "Wobblies," and eventually went to Russia. He was buried in the Kremlin as a hero in the "class war" preached by the Communists.

William E. Borah achieved a national reputation for his able (though unsuccessful) prosecution of Big Bill Haywood in 1907. He spent the rest of his life in the United States Senate where his oratory and independence were admired.

James H. Hawley was already a noted Idaho attorney when he teamed with Borah in the Haywood case. He served as Mayor of Boise and Governor of Idaho.

William Dudley "Big Bill" Haywood has been described as "massive, one-eyed, with a face like a scarred mountain." Because of his disfigurement he always posed in profile.

ISHS

Big Bill Haywood once commanded the allegiance of thousands of miners like these. He himself had started working in Utah copper mines when he was only 10 years old.

Many people took snapshots of the Liberty Bell's visit to Boise on July 12, 1915. Here are some of them.

A Revered Visitor

 Idaho's replica of the liberty Bell, which stands today in front of the Capitol, arrived in the state on May 30, 1950. After touring small towns and cities, it was officially accepted by Gov. Charles A. Robins in a Boise ceremony on the evening of July 5.

A parade, made up mostly of men and women who had been active in war bond sales, and of those in charge of the peacetime U.S. Savings Bond program, escorted the symbol of American Independence to the statehouse.

The small crowd that attended was but a shadow of the tremendous turnout Idaho had given to the real Liberty Bell 35 years before. In July, 1915, World War I was raging across the Atlantic. German submarines had become a principal topic of conversation, after the sinking of the *Lusitania* in May, with the loss of many American lives. President Wilson had issued a series of sharp warnings to the German government, and the German reply was being awaited uneasily.

Most Americans hoped we could stay out of the war, but German actions and a flood of British propaganda had succeeded in stirring up a great deal of patriotic emotion, even in far-away Idaho.

It was just at this moment that the famed Liberty Bell came to the Gem State, accompanied by a delegation from the Philadelphia city council. On a whirlwind schedule that gave the councilmen little time for sleep, the great American symbol was shown to millions who never expected to see it outside its usual Independence Hall home.

Governor and Mrs. Moses Alexander met the train bearing the bell at Weston, Idaho, and accompanied it across the state to Boise, and then on to Weiser.

At Pocatello, 15,000 had turned out to see it. Trains passing through that railroad junction were held up in order that passengers could also take advantage of the once-in-a-lifetime opportunity.

At Shoshone, although the hour was 1:30 in the morning, hundreds of people had been called out by the fire bell, and were eagerly waiting when the train with its hallowed cargo arrived.

"The townspeople turned out as if it were midday," read the report, and went on to say that hundreds had come to town from as far away as Hailey. "Little children were borne in arms to touch

117

the bell as their sires and the older folks, gathered at the railroad side, uncovered and cheered lustily.''

The same scene was repeated at Mountain Home at 4 a.m., where ''numerous automobiles and carriages brought residents of the surrounding country to the early morning party.''

In Boise, the crowd began to gather at 6:30, ''flocking down Eighth, Ninth, and Tenth streets and swarming around the depot and park.'' The depot, on Front street then, became the center of a crowd that filled every foot of space for two blocks in all directions.

The schedule only permitted a stop of 45 minutes in Idaho's little capital city, but the crowd of 15,000 was able to file by in an orderly fashion on both sides of the train.

Most small children were held up by their parents to touch the bell, and a great many were urged to kiss it.

''Let them come,'' said one of the Philadelphia policemen guarding the bell. ''It's good for them, and it don't hurt the bell . . . it belongs as much to them as to their elders, and they'll never forget having touched it.''

At Nampa, 2,000 people had gathered in the hope that the train would stop there. Since it wasn't scheduled to do so, it didn't. Caldwell was luckier, somehow managing to hold the Liberty Bell captive for 25 minutes.

The Great War

 September 24, 1917, was a day marked by "an upwelling of sentiment and patriotism that will never be forgotten," according to a *Statesman* editorial of the time. It was the day the Second Idaho Volunteers left for the East and eventual service in France in World War I.

Three photographs from that day help bring the occasion back to life. The first shows the crowd of thousands that choked Tenth Street from the Idanha Hotel to Front Street where the Idaho men boarded trains for Camp Green, North Carolina.

Although it had been promised that bells would ring and whistles blow the moment the men left Boise Barracks, in order that Boiseans, friends, and relatives from the country might give them a suitable patriotic sendoff, as a matter of fact the marching troops were nearly downtown that damp September morning before it was realized that this was indeed the long-awaited departure day.

Then the crowd gathered with surprising speed, engulfing passing cars and leaving them abandoned islands in a sea of strong emotion.

Military censorship of troop movements was a novelty then, and the papers showed some confusion as to just how to handle their responsibilities to the home folks and to the nation at war at the same time. This was no easy task, since the Second Idaho consisted of 2,000 officers and men. There were vast numbers of civilians and many people had failed to get early enough notice of the departure. Many wives and sweethearts of men leaving Idaho that day waited around the railroad yard for 12 hours or more, hoping to catch a glimpse of their own soldiers, not knowing the schedule.

During their month in North Carolina the Idaho men apparently got along well with the local inhabitants. One report said it had been learned that the "wild westerners would make life hideous for the peaceful southerners," but there was genuine regret at seeing them leave.

On October 25 they arrived in New York, where they became part of the famed Sunset Division made up of men from western states. There was some disappointment over this, as most of the men had hoped to go to war under the Idaho colors. It is even said that some of the officers wept.

While Idaho's young men waited restlessly on Long Island for

When the 2nd Idaho Infantry left Boise for training camp in North Carolina in 1917, thousands crowded Tenth and Front Streets to see them off.

Coffee and sandwiches were served to Idaho troops in the Front Street yards before their train pulled out. Spirits were high as these young Idahoans set off on their great adventure. Some would not come back.

Blanket rolls on shoulders, these Idaho Infantrymen were about to board their train when this shot was taken. It was a day to remember.

their boat trip to France, people at home were equally restless and stirred up by the new and frenzied activities the war had thrust upon them.

Not only were the front pages plastered with glaring headlines about events overseas, but Liberty Loan drives, Red Cross drives, food conservation drives, and even "tobacco for our boys" drives were carried on everywhere.

The public was urged by a Boise movie house to remember two things: "Buy a Liberty Bond and Go to the Majestic." Among feature attractions at the movies that fall were William S. Hart in "The Cold Deck" and "The Last Days of Pompeii." The Chicago White Sox won the World Series four games to two over the New York Giants, and in Boise recruiters worked hard to meet quotas.

Astonishing as it seems, Bruneau topped the list of volunteers with 26 to Boise's 23, and a headline said "Villages Most Loyal." Another recruiting story was headed "Buckaroos in Demand by Uncle Samuel."

In the general patriotic mood of the times, freedom of speech and opinion were considerably curtailed. A German-born farmer in Star was visited by a "committee" which made him grovel in the dust and kiss the American flag. He was also made to paint his hay derrick red, white, and blue, and forced to contribute $50 to the Y.M.C.A. drive. Rewards were offered for the exposure of draft-dodgers, and a screaming page one banner headline proclaimed "Government Plans to Exterminate the Anti-war Propaganda."

The men of the former Second Idaho Volunteers sailed for France on November 26, 1917, as part of the Sunset Division. For many still living in Idaho today, their departure from Boise that September was truly a moment never forgotten.

Charles A. Lindbergh posed with Governor H.C.
Baldridge on May 21, 1927.

Lucky Lindy

On Saturday, May 21, 1927, downtown Boise was buzzing with excitement. In those days, just about everybody had to work on Saturdays, at least in the morning, but that day nothing much got done between 11 in the morning and 2:30 in the afternoon.

Every Boisean had his thoughts, hopes, and prayers tuned in to a distant airplane somewhere 6,000 miles away headed for Paris, piloted by a slim and boyish Minnesotan named Charles A. Lindbergh.

Crowds of people waited in front of *The Statesman* bulletin board at Sixth and Main for reports, fearing that the brave young airmail pilot and his silver monoplane *Spirit of St. Louis* had gone down in the Atlantic. Many had already failed in such attempts, and several had never been heard from again. What was unique about Lindbergh's flight was that he was flying the Atlantic alone in a single-engine plane, and no one had ever done that before.

When the word came that Lindbergh had landed at LeBourget Field in Paris, as 100,000 Frenchmen rioted to see him and to touch him, Boise and the rest of America went slightly crazy, too.

Senator Borah, with his usual eloquence, summed it up like this: "The spirit of American youth incarnate — the spirit which charms and subdues to its purpose all things. That is what the feat of Charlie Lindbergh means to me. Nothing could be more simple, sincere and courageous. It ought to lift every American boy into the atmosphere of the heroic — life is worthwhile."

To Boise, which had seen the inauguration of Varney Air Lines' mail service here only the year before, the pilots who flew the mail in all kinds of weather in their flimsy biplanes were already heroes, and Lindy had flown the mail in the Midwest. Only a month before Lindbergh's epic flight, another young airmail pilot had been killed in a crash at King Hill while flying to Boise. William Sandborn was his name, and his fate made Idahoans all the more aware of the dangers Lindbergh faced in crossing the Atlantic alone.

New York papers began predicting that "Lucky Lindy" had a million dollars within his grasp already, if he would only cash in on his sudden fame. Everyone wanted to hire him — newspapers, the movies, and even vaudeville theaters. Lindy rejected all such schemes, but agreed to go on tour with the *Spirit of St. Louis* to further the cause of aviation in America.

"Lucky Lindy" was a national hero when he landed the Spirit of St. Louis in Boise before thousands of Idahoans from miles around. He later autographed this Johnson & Son photo for Leo J. Falk, left. Governor Baldridge and Mayor Walter F. Hansen are in center.

Boise had made aviation history the year before Lindbergh's visit when Varney Airlines began commercial airmail service here in April, 1926.

On September 4, 1927, 40,000 Idahoans gathered at Boise's airport (located where Boise State University is now) to greet Lindbergh. Since Boise's population was 21,000 at that time, it is apparent that the rural areas and other towns in southern Idaho were also well represented.

When the speck in the sky over Table Rock finally appeared against a big, fleecy cloud, people were hardly able to contain themselves. After a graceful series of controlled acrobatics, *Spirit of St. Louis* touched down in Idaho, and the great moment had arrived.

"Then he stepped out and stood — long, slender, bronzed, handsome, towering, with a pose that would have been gawkiness except for that wistfulness which turned it into grace." *The Statesman's* writer captured beautifully the "Lindy image" that has survived the years — the image shown in the photographs on these pages.

Leo J. Falk, Governor H.C. Baldridge, and Mayor Walter F. Hansen are shown with "The Lone Eagle" in one of the photographs made by Ansgar Johnson, Sr., that day in 1927. Two prints in the Idaho Historical Society files were donated by Mrs. Leo J. Falk. One bears the autograph of Charles A. Lindbergh. "X-211" and "Ryan," builder of the *Spirit of St. Louis*, can be seen on the tail of the famous plane in the background.

Governor Baldridge drops a letter into the slot of a Varney airmail plane. Senator Borah is at left, Mayor Hansen at right.

The Spirit of St. Louis *seconds after landing at Boise's airport beside the river — now the site of Boise State University.*

ENTERTAINMENT

ISHS 964

Boise's first large space suitable for theatrical performances was Good Templars' Hall, near the corner of Sixth and Main. The temperance lodge built it in 1869. This view was taken on July 4, 1890, the day after Boise became capital of the 43rd state in the Union.

Theatrical Pioneers

Theatrical performances were much-treasured events in early Boise. Often many months passed between visits of professional troupes to Idaho's scattered and isolated mining camps and small towns, and people turned out in force to enjoy the novelty of some culture and entertainment.

The pages of the pioneer newspapers devote much space to these highlights in the life of communities where even dog fights and drunken brawls passed for entertainment. Some accounts suggest, however, that the audiences did not behave as well as the editors might have wished:

"We think the crowd that generally assembles in the 'pit' of our places of amusement the most badly behaved of any we ever saw. They seem perfectly regardless of what is going on in front on the stage, and amuse themselves by yelling and whooping whenever the spirit moves them.

"Not content with the continual cracking of peanuts, and demands for more from time to time in loud vociferations, but they must needs indulge in unearthly shrieks, resembling the coyote or Snake Indian, interrupting and confusing the actors, and preventing the more orderly of the audience from hearing anything of the play in progress.

"We have no doubt the 'boys' intend such outbreaks of feeling as complimentary applause, and that it is offered in a generous and kindly spirit, but for our part we hope hereafter there will be less of it."

The above was written in 1870, when Boise was a rough and tough frontier town, but nearly 20 years later audiences were still arousing editorial wrath: "Taylor, the Capital hall man, when another show comes to town, should engage the services of a first-class foolkiller, with a big club, to take a quiet walk through the audience and thin it out some. The conduct of certain parties at the DeMoss concert on Wednesday night was simply disgraceful."

What kind of shows were available in a community like Boise in early days? The variety is impressive, and in some cases surprisingly cultured. The versatility of the traveling artists was also remarkable. As an illustration, let us examine the Boise visit of the Carrie Chapman Troupe, which offered its first performance on April 13, 1871, and remained for over a month. Most of these per-

This artist's conception of the Sonna Opera House interior was published in 1890. James A. Pinney was manager of the theater at the time, but would build his own Columbia Theater two years later.

formances were held in Good Templars' Hall, then the finest theatrical facility in Idaho. Our illustration shows it many years later when decay had set in, but gives an idea of its size and style. The building, constructed in the spring of 1870, stood near the northeast corner of Sixth and Main Streets. It took its name from the temperance organization that built it.

In addition to a repertoire of 12 separate plays, ranging from serious drama to light comedy, the Chapman troupe regularly offered interludes of singing and dancing. Comment was made upon the handsome costumes and fine effect produced in these adjuncts to the main show. Comedy sketches featured "delineations of negro character," and the song and dance included a double routine by "Miss Carrie," the star, with her husband, and banjo solo "loudly cheered and encored." Play titles still sound intriguing today: *The Doublebedded Room, The Spectre Bridegroom, The Miser's Legacy,* and *How Far Is It To The Next Ranch?,* obviously a western.

When the regular list of plays had been performed, and the most successful given a second showing, the company put on a minstrel show, featuring the standard characters of Tambourine and Bones.

Even a Shakespearian recitation was thrown in, as the Chapman Troupe pulled out all the stops to get a few more Boise dollars for the road. On their way to other territories, they made stops in both the Owyhee and Boise Basin mining districts.

Spectacular Effects

A definite trend in traveling theater in the United States at the end of the 19th century was to subordinate plot and acting to technical effects. A number of shrewd producers found that there were more people willing to pay to see spectacle and novelty than to watch serious drama, and since there was always a shortage of top-flight talent willing to do one-night stands, it was good business from that standpoint, too.

Audiences in the hinterlands certainly knew the difference between a good dramatic performance and a poor one, and the reviewers were hardly gentle. A performance of *Avenged* at Sonna's Opera House in 1892 was called "a disgusting fake." In 1894, the new Columbia Theater was packed on the night of November 29, "for a miserably poor performance of Harriet Beecher Stowe's great work, *Uncle Tom's Cabin*. The piece was literally butchered. It was nothing short of a crime to disappoint such a magnificent house . . .".

Perhaps it was safer to offer novelties in stage effects that would at least appeal to the American love of mechanical ingenuity. *The Fast Mail*, produced in October, 1894, at the Columbia, featured no less than ten sets of special scenery: "Flight of the fast mail; Niagara Falls by moonlight, with boiling mist; practical working engine and 14 freight cars, with illuminated caboose; the Dago dive; realistic river scene and steamboat, explosion, and other startling effects."

The Statesman's reviewer noted "the play is made a great deal on the blood and thunder order, with sundry explosions thrown in to fill the house with choking smoke. There is nothing in the piece that calls for much acting. The hero has only to fall into the traps laid by the villain and wait until the weeping heroine comes along to snatch him from the jaws of death." The review is definitely a favorable one, however, for the scenery was hailed as "far above average," and the Niagara Falls scene as "perfect."

In December, a play called *The County Fair* featured a race of thoroughbred horses on the stage, using real horses and clever illusions. An old barn with real hay, (real horses again, of course), a husking bee, and a "rustic dance" were also features of this production.

In 1896, Steve Brodie, who had become famous by jumping off the Brooklyn Bridge, came to Boise in a road show featuring that

The Columbia Theater opened December 12, 1892, with a performance of Shakespeare's As You Like It starring Julia Marlowe, a big name at the time.

Pinney's Columbia Theater, 1892-1908, was decorated with ceiling art featuring famous dramatists and performers. The place of honor, however, was reserved for James A. Pinney's portrait, center.

For dramatic impact it was hard to beat the 1909
appearance at the Pinney of more than 30 real
live Eskimos from North Head, Siberia.
Apparently the whole village went on the road at
the behest of some enterprising showman.

The Pinney Theater of 1908 was James Pinney's
last major venture. It succeeded his Columbia
across the street on Jefferson.

great publicity stunt. "The Brooklyn Bridge scene was realistic, but the gallant rescue of the drowning heroine was purely mechanical, both in design and effect."

The press was much more impressed the following day when it turned out that two members of the Brodie cast had been arrested for breaking in a door at the Columbia Theater. This escapade was headlined "Bowery in Real Life," and called it a "safe cracker's rehearsal."

At about this time Boise saw her first motion pictures — a development that was eventually to surpass anything in the way of realism the stage had produced. These early movies, billed as "Edison's Original Electric Moving Pictures," were also heavily oriented toward effects rather than drama. Hailing an 1898 performance as the best yet seen in Boise, *The Statesman* reviewer said that the crowd had especially liked *A Snowballing Match*, a *Surf Scene on the Irish Coast*, and a *Spanish Bullfight*.

In 1899, "a new water scene was introduced, one in which some people fall into the waves. It was so realistic that a little girl in the audience cried out in tones of fright, 'Oh mama, they are drowning!'"

The Great Train Robbery was not shown in Boise until September, 1904, on the wall of the old Main Street firehouse. "The pictures were punctuated with pistol shots and were rendered very realistic," said the happy reviewer.

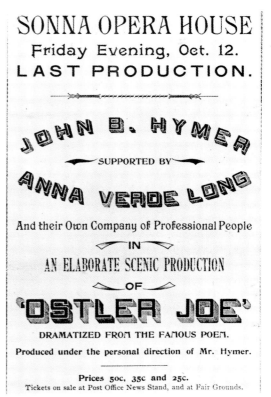

SONNA OPERA HOUSE
Friday Evening, Oct. 12.
LAST PRODUCTION.

JOHN B. HYMER
➤ SUPPORTED BY ➤
ANNA VERDE LONG

And their Own Company of Professional People

➤ IN ➤

AN ELABORATE SCENIC PRODUCTION

➤ OF ➤

'OSTLER JOE'

DRAMATIZED FROM THE FAMOUS POEM.

Produced under the personal direction of Mr. Hymer.

Prices 50c, 35c and 25c.
Tickets on sale at Post Office News Stand, and at Fair Grounds.

This program of an 1888 performance in Peter Sonna's new opera house at Ninth and Main is one of the few to survive from early days. (An ostler was a caretaker for horses and mules).

Fire curtains in theaters were long decorated with historical or scenic paintings, and the ads of local businesses. This was the Pinney's in about 1912.

Boise's Columbia Band was active for a decade.
Here they pose in a cottonwood grove near
Riverside Park.

Those Beautiful Bands

 Band music has been popular with Boiseans for more than a century. It wouldn't have been a real Fourth of July without one, nor could any parade have been half as exciting without the musical accompaniment that only a rousing brass band could give it.

Traveling bands sometimes visited frontier towns, but most of the time the towns did very well for themselves with local talent. As early as April, 1869, Boise had a brass band. It probably wasn't too good, but *The Statesman* reported that it was "rapidly improving."

The Army's Fort Boise would have bands later, but since troops in the Sixties came and went, and since there were times when the whole garrison numbered only a handful of soldiers, there were many years without music there.

The town band was a feature of most Idaho mining towns, as well as her capital city. On Holidays they performed at parades, gave concerts, and played for dances that lasted all night. Sometimes, they played just for the fun of it, creating their own special occasion. This the Boise band did on a balmy night in June of 1870, when they serenaded Governor Ballard.

In May, 1876, there was considerable local interest when a unique touring band came to town. Professor Boulton's Ladies' Cornet Band paraded through the streets of Boise in full uniform. The men thought it daring; some women may have thought it immodest. This parade had the function of a circus parade, helping to stir up interest and ticket sales for a performance to follow.

German-born Alois Steidel was the organizer and leader of many of Boise's early musical groups. He was described in July, 1875, as "an accomplished cornet and clarionet [sic] player" who was "getting up" a brass band and giving lessons to several young men. "There is nothing the people would sooner hear than a good brass band, and we say, all speed and success to the organization."

By October of 1880 the *Idaho World* of Idaho City could say "Boise City has one of the best brass bands on the coast, outside of California." The Capital Brass Band of 1882, with many of the same players, adopted a schedule of rates for performances: "Street parades — for National holidays, $100; afternoon and evening, first hour, $25; each additional hour, $10; funeral services, $40; Serenades, evening, $25; Sociables and festivals, $15;

Some of the pioneer musicians who played in Boise's Philharmonic Orchestra of 1887 also performed in the city's brass bands over the years. Clarinetist Alois Steidel, center standing, was the founder and leader of most of them. The string players in this group played for dances, but probably never marched with a band.

each additional night, $10."

The Statesman explained that these were very reasonable rates, since the organization had "considerable expenses . . . for rent, light, fuel and continual replenishment of new music, which is very expensive." The paper said if the people wished to have a band they should "do all in their power to sustain the enterprise."

By 1885, another group, calling itself the Boise City Brass Band, had been organized. All of these amateur groups eventually faded out of existence, but new ones were started to replace them. A Boys' Band, organized in 1897, entertained the community for several years with weekly dances at G.A.R. Hall, the proceeds of which paid for uniforms and instruments. This group also played from the balcony of the Overland Hotel at 8th and Main and, in April, 1898, for prisoners at the Idaho Penitentiary east of town.

Boise's most famous band at the turn of the century was the Columbia. It lasted longer than any of the others. For many years it played regular summer concerts, even taking to automobiles for a musical serenade of the city in 1907. The Columbia shared billing at the Intermountain fair with top visiting bands from out of town, including those of Payette and DeLamar, Idaho, and the Held Military Band of Salt Lake City.

ISHS 62-168.3

*The Boise City Band seems to be carrying a May
pole canopy in this undated photograph. Each
man seems to be attached to one of the ribbons.
The setting looks like Grove Street.*

When the Circus Came to Town

Show business had a glamor that residents of Boise and neighboring valleys could not resist in the summer of 1902. They flocked to the city with their horses and buggies, and on the special excursion trains that the Oregon Short Line offered for every big event.

In addition to newly opened Riverside Park and Pinney's tent theater, the Pavilion, there were the other old stand-bys: the Natatorium and the Sonna and Columbia theatres.

What really drew the largest crowds were the circuses. Boise obviously enjoyed a good reputation as a "show town," and the big ones all came here. Ringling Brothers came annually for many years, playing to near capacity every time. The favorite circus grounds were in open fields on the south side of Front Street. Here the special trains all of the circuses used could unload directly from the O.S.L. siding and be set up in a matter of hours. The first day invariably started with a big parade through town at 10 a.m., followed by afternoon and evening performances.

The season of 1902 started out with Gentry Brothers' Famous Shows featuring "325 animal actors." Their tent had a seating capacity of 3,000. Less than a week after the Gentry show left, the Great Pan-American Shows arrived. Their train, consisting of 18 cars, was unloaded in the early hours of May 7. A mile long parade was advertised, and their star attraction was "Rajah, the largest elephant that walks the earth." (According to the circus artist's posters, Rajah was about the height of a two-story building, but that was show-biz.)

When the Pan-American shows left town, two local girls tried to run away from home to join the circus. Mattie and Harcia May might have made it, too, but their unhappy fathers got so ugly about the whole thing that the circus people pointed out their hiding place. Harcia May was only 13, so it is likely the circus couldn't use her anyhow.

On August 2, the advance guard for Ringling Brothers arrived in town in the form of "Advertising Car No. 3." A crew of 15 men set out to paste up their colorful posters on every fence, wall, and barn in the valley. In a few days their newspaper ads also began to appear, featuring that season "the only giraffe known to exist in the world."

The theme of "this is your last chance" was used in advertising Buffalo Bill's Wild West show when it came to Boise valley. Only

Newspaper ads of 1902 were imaginative and totally unrestrained in their claims — but few in Boise could resist them.

FIRST, LAST AND ONLY VISIT
THE BIGGEST AND BEST OF ALL
BOISE CITY NOT UNTIL MONDAY AUG. 18
"AU REVOIR, BUT NOT GOODBYE."
WILL POSITIVE GO T O EUROPE THIS FALL,
BUT THIS YEAR IT WILL TOUR THE AMERICAN CONTINENT.

FROM OCEAN TO OCEAN
Visiting the Principal Cities and Greater Railway Centers Only, as a Parting
Salute to the Great Nation Which Gave It Birth.

AND CONGRESS OF ROUGH RIDERS OF THE WORLD
Now in the Zenith of its Overwhelming and Triumphant Success, Presenting
a Program of Marvelous Merit and Introducing the

....WORLD'S MOUNTED WARRIORS.....
Such as INDIANS, SOLDIERS OF THE AMERICAN, ENGLISH, GERMAN,
RUSSIAN AND CUBAN ARMIES, FULLY EQUIPPED AND

READY FOR WAR
AN EXHIBITION THAT TEACHES BUT DOES NOT IMITATE.

THESE ARE THE MEN WHO DO AND DARE
AND THESE ARE THE EVENTS IN THE ACTION:
A GRAND REVIEW OF ALL NATIONS—A RACE OF RACES, In which Cow-
boys, Cossacks, Mexicans, Gauchos and American Indians Participate—
ARTILLERY DRILL BY VETERANS — A "ROUND-UP" ON THE
PLAINS, with Incidental Events—PONY EXPRESS RIDING—GROUPS
OF MEXICAN HORSEMEN AND LASSO EXPERTS — CELEBRATED
CRACK SHOTS AND NOTED MARKSMEN—REAL ARABIAN HORSE-
MEN AND ATHLETES—LIFE SAVING DRILLS, by Veteran Members
of the U. S. Life-Saving Service—GENUINE COSSACKS FROM THE
CAUCASUS OF RUSSIA—INDIAN BOYS IN FAVORITE PASTIMES—
COWBOY FUN WITH THE BUCKING BRONCHOS—U. S. CAVALRY
DRILLS AND MILITARY EXERCISES—THE FAMOUS DEADWOOD
STAGE COACH, Attack, Repulse and Victory—MOMENTS WITH THE
BOLAS THROWERS—ROUGH RIDERS AND NATIVE GAUCHOS.

COLONEL W. F. CODY, (Buffalo Bill)
IN FEATS OF MARKMANSHIP—A BUFFALO HUNT IN THE FAR WEST
—A HERD OF REAL BUFFALO, the Last of Their Race—GRAND MIL-
ITARY MANEUVERS—EPISODE S O FCAMP LIFE, with all of its Hu-
mor and Hardships—THE BIVOU AC AT NIGHT—ASSEMBLY OF THE
ALLIED ARMIES, incidental Drill and Action—REALISTIC SCENES
"ON THE FIRING LINE"—ALL THE EXCITING ELEMENTS OF AC-
TUAL WARFARE AND BATTLE —IN WIHCH "OLD GLORY" AL-
WAYS WAVES TRIUMPHANT— SEE IT WHILE YOU MAY! ENJOY
IT WHILE YOU CAN!

GRAND REVIEW OF THE ROUGH RIDERS
IN STREET CAVALCADE AT 9 A. M. ON DATE OF EXHIBITION. THE
WHOLE CULMINATING WITH THE GREAT MILITARY SPECTA-
CLE OF

about one third of the ad is reproduced here, but is enough to give the idea. How the eyes of small boys and girls must have shone when they read through the seemingly endless list of wonders that the great show offered. How they must have pressured their parents to go (if they had any sales resistance left after reading the ad themselves.)

The reporter who described Buffalo Bill's triumphant ride through Boise's streets certainly had succumbed completely to the glamor of the famous showman: "First came a drum corps of 12 pieces followed by Col. Cody, to whom the crowds gave repeated ovations. Under his jaunty broad-brimmed hat there gleamed in kindliness eyes that have seen wonders worked on these western plains; eyes that have seen roses bloom where blood was spilled, peace smile where war frowned, plenty bless where famine robbed, knowledge rule where superstition held sway — in short, the birth and growth of civilization in the great west."

The circus parade was the only part of the show that was absolutely free. Boiseans turned out in droves to see "ponderous pachyderms" and magnificent wagons of scarlet and gold.

Elephants paraded past the Idanha corner of Tenth and Main. C.C. Anderson's Golden Rule store shows in background (later home of J.C. Penney).

The bandstand and dancing pavilion at Riverside Park were tucked in among the cottonwoods. The all-purpose center of amusements opened on June 26, 1902.

An undated Photo of a Boise baseball team about to entrain for a game. Opponents early in this century could have included the Weiser Kids, *with Walter Johnson pitching, the* Emmett Prunepickers, *the* Payette Melon Eaters, Caldwell Champions, Nampa Beetdiggers, *or* Mountain Home Dudes. *Boise's team was called the* Senators *in that era.*

The Summer of 1902

"Progress," so-called, is never without its losses. This is especially evident when researching the kinds of entertainment available to the people of Boise Valley at the turn of the century. Although they had no television or radio, and only occasionally the flickering pioneer movies, people of those days enjoyed live entertainment in a variety and richness surprising for a small frontier city.

If you were a sport fan living in Boise, Payette, or Weiser valleys, you could watch semi-professional baseball a couple of times a week. Moreover, if you wanted to follow your favorite team to neighboring towns to root them on, you could go at special excursion rates on the train. The train ride itself could qualify as entertainment, since you could walk around while traveling, visit from one end of the train to the other, eat, drink, or just enjoy the scenery from comfortable seats, through large windows. Your town band might even be aboard to serenade the fans on the way to and from the game.

In the summer of 1902, as we have described elsewhere, three circuses came to the valley. They came in style, in huge special trains of their own, and each started things off with grand free parades. In July, 1902, Boise planned its own "big top," when James A. Pinney ordered a 1,500-seat tent from the local Pioneer Co., to be set up at Eighth and Jefferson near his Columbia Theatre. The Pavilion Theatre, as it was called, opened at the beginning of August with a capable stock company in a performance of *The Henrietta*. The reviews were enthusiastic, praising the actors, the handsome new scenery, and especially the fine orchestra.

Riverside Park was also built in the summer of 1902, opening with the Elks Carnival on June 26. The huge, old cottonwoods along the river were carefully thinned to make attractive grounds for a "mammoth dancing pavilion" and a baseball diamond. One of the regular shows valley residents could see there that summer consisted of eight separate acts, featuring Matsuda's Japanese jugglers, acrobats, and equilibrists, Dalton & Lewis in a sketch called *Rival Editors* (with dancing in wooden shoes), and Dorr & Stanley in *Songs the Boys Are Singing in the Camps Tonight*. There was also, of course, a live orchestra that played throughout the performance.

Sonna's Opera House, the Columbia Theater, and the famous Natatorium were also active that summer, and the Columbia

Special trains were run from Boise's Front Street station on the Idaho Central Railroad to most out-of-town baseball games. This 1893 depot stood at the foot of Tenth Street. It was the scene of many historic departures.

SUNDAY
BALL GAME
Aug. 3 Only.

New England Bloomers
vs.
Riverside Park

The Eastern Girls against the Western Boys in a red hot game.

The Bloomers' famous pitcher Miss Grace Wood, will positively appear in the box.

The New England Bloomers disappointed at least some in their Boise audience because they weren't pretty enough — but they won the game.

Band played regular concerts downtown for the pleasure of the citizens. (You could also listen to the Salvation Army band on the streets, and get a sermon thrown in.) The Natatorium featured swimming, concerts, and public dancing.

An unusual sporting event of August, 1902, was the arrival in town of the New England Bloomers, a female baseball team. Arrangements were made for them to play a local amateur outfit called the Lobsters, and the surprising result was a victory for the Bloomers, 10-9.

The Statesman's sports reporter was furious. He pointed out that the Bloomers got by through having two first-class men players at catcher and shortstop. The girls relayed their throws to the shortstop, who made all the plays. While admitting that Grace Wood, the Bloomer pitcher was pretty good, the reporter called the whole affair "rotten" and "punk," and said "those who remained away from the ball park have every reason to be shaking hands with themselves."

In a singularly unchivalrous concluding remark, the irate reporter said, "there might be some excuse for the exhibition if the members of the team from New England (?) were even fairly good looking."

BUILDING A CITY
The Fight Against Fire

One of the turning points in the history of Boise came with the fulfillment of a long-held dream — the formation of a fire department, and efforts to secure the capital city's first fire engine.

It marked the difference between a ramshackle frontier town in a constant danger of destruction from fire, and a new era of growth, with the hope that fires could now be controlled. It also led to a new consciousness of the necessity of replacing wooden buildings with brick and stone.

After more than a decade of unsuccessful attempts at permanent organization, and several small but costly fires, the Boise City Fire Company was formed at a meeting on January 24, 1876. Twenty-eight men joined the association. Their first official act was to appoint a fund-raising committee for fire-fighting equipment. This, and subsequent meetings that year, were held in the Turn Verein Hall on the southeast corner of Sixth and Main. This old wooden hall was also rented by the Idaho legislature from time to time in those days, since there was no permanent home for government yet.

On February 15, a constitution and by-laws were adopted, and a slate of officers was elected from prominent citizens. They were: Lafayette Cartee, president; Milton Kelly, owner and editor of *The Statesman*, vice president; A. Wolters, secretary, and John Lemp, treasurer.

The first business transacted was the commissioning of a hook and ladder truck, to be built locally by Marston and Donohue, blacksmiths. The cost of this hand-drawn vehicle, with hooks, ladders, and ropes, was $300. In April, the fire company paid $325 for the old wooden blacksmith shop formerly used by George Washington Stilts. This building was midway between Sixth and Seventh on the south side of Main.

In May, the first of many fund-raising activities was announced — a Firemen's Ball to take place on the ninth of June. Firemen were told to get their uniforms ready in time for the dance. Black trousers, red shirts, and special belts and hats made up the colorful regalia. Interest was now high, and 56 men had signed up as volunteer firemen. That first ball was described as "brilliantly successful," and produced a long news story about the activities of the evening.

James A. Pinney, while in Chicago that summer, purchased a

Boise's volunteer fire department frequently drilled on city streets. This 1895 photo was taken at the corner of Seventh and Main. Had it been a parade the boys would have been in their classy uniforms, but for equipment drills they "came as they were."

Boise's first fire station was a former blacksmith shop on the south side of Main between Sixth and Seventh. This picture was taken in 1879 shortly after the Silsby steam pumper came to town.

400 pound bell for the fire hall. It was mid-August when it arrived and was hung on a temporary wooden frame 22 feet high.

The town was now taking a lively interest in the progress being made, and was delighted when the company held its first parade with the new hook and ladder truck. In October, the City Council passed an ordinance re-organizing the department under men who would actually do the work, replacing the "honorary" officers elected earlier.

Another "Grand Ball" was held December 12, 1876, "for the purpose of raising funds to purchase a fire engine." "The firemen, dressed in full regalia, presented a fine appearance," said the paper on this occasion. "Their red shirts, dark pantaloons . . . and palpitating hearts were in beautiful contrast with the elaborate dresses and the charmingly graceful and self-possessed manner of the ladies."

It was to take seven Firemen's balls over the next three years to raise the first thousand dollars toward the purchase of the engine. Boise's first fire engine arrived on the afternoon of July 15, 1879. It had taken 17 days to haul the heavy steamer over the Kelton Road from Utah, and it must have made quite a sight crossing the sagebrush plains as part of a train of freight wagons.

The Silsby, "bright as a new silver dollar," was viewed with pride and delight by the whole community. She was labeled *Boise City*, in a handsome scroll sign, and was hailed as being "a model

Even after a professional fire department was formed in 1902, the old volunteers continued to meet socially for many years. They had held fund-raising balls for so long that they were reluctant to give up the popular annual get-togethers. This one of 1911 was held in the G.A.R. Hall.

ISHS 1239-B

The city's Idaho Street fire station was next door to City Hall. These volunteers posed proudly in about 1895.

Members of Boise City Engine Company Number One were proud of their dark blue uniforms and their shiny engine, Boise City.

of workmanship, as good as any in San Francisco of the same size."

On July 17, 1879, at six o'clock in the evening, the fire engine was run down to Grove Street for its first official public demonstration. The hose was strung out 500 feet "opposite C. Jacobs' residence." A light note on the historic occasion was furnished when "there was some carelessness in throwing the water where the ladies and gentlemen were standing, that caused an occasional scattering of the crowd. "It was fun to some, but unpleasant to those who got wet, especially the ladies who came elegantly dressed."

On Tuesday, July 22, the company paraded the new *Boise City* throughout the town, ending with a demonstration that included shooting water twenty feet over the top of the Methodist Church steeple. The pumper was placed at the Grove Street ditch and accomplished the feat by sending water through 900 feet of hose.

That evening "the elite of the city" danced "until the small hours of the night" in celebration of Boise's arrival as a metropolis with a steam fire engine of its very own.

The city had several small fires in early days, but miraculously escaped a really big one. Damaged wooden buildings in this 1887 photo were replaced with brick ones.

ISHS 78-64.1/b

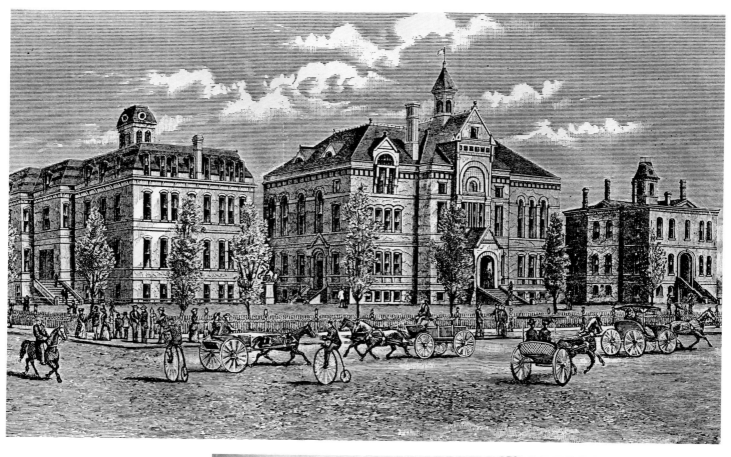

When Idaho's volunteers returned from the Philippines in 1889, the old capitol was richly decorated with red, white and blue. The iron fence in foreground now surrounds the Historical Society's Pioneer Village in Julia Davis Park.

At Last a Capitol

 Idaho's Territorial Capitol building of 1885-86 was an imposing structure remarkably different in size, style and color from the present State Capitol. It occupied part of the ground now covered by the House of Representatives' wing, and had some rather interesting public buildings as neighbors.

A wood engraving published in 1887 shows a compressed view of Capitol Square at the end of the Eighties. On the left is Boise's Central School. On the right is the old Ada County Courthouse. The lively scene has been embellished by the artist with a variety of Idahoans passing by this display of architectural grandeur — for such it was at the time.

In addition to pedestrians, this picture shows an interesting variety of other modes of transportation. From left to right are a horseman, a high-wheel cyclist, a couple in a two-wheel cart, another cycle, a wagon, a wicker cart with canopy, and a surrey with a fringe on top.

Barely visible is another famous Boise horseman — the Charles Ostner statue of George Washington which then stood west of the capitol on the grounds. When the artist of our engraving decided to push all of the buildings closer together to get them into one compact view, he had to put the Ostner statue in the schoolyard.

The architect of Idaho's capitol was E.E. Myers of Detroit. He won a design competition with what he called a Norman structure — Norman being synonymous at the time with the newly-popular Romanesque style, a revival of the middle ages. A number of other Boise buildings would be Romanesque revival in the next twenty years.

Thomas Finnegan received the first contract for work on the new statehouse. He was a masonry contractor awarded the basement excavation and stone work for the foundation. Later, Finnegan supervised all of the brick work for the rest of the structure. Commenting on the active scene at the construction site, *The Statesman* noted that "the sound of the mason's mallet and chisel makes a contrast with the silence that was wont to prevail there.

"At night the place looks like a thickly populated graveyard, the numerous pieces of cut and uncut stone having an appearance uncanny in the extreme." In July 1885, James Flanagan was awarded the contract for supplying brick at $10 per thousand. It

When the Idaho legislature and its staff assembled for this picture in the Territorial Capitol, spittoons were a prominent part of the furniture.

The Republican-dominated Idaho Senate of 1909 decorated its chambers with flag-festooned portraits of William McKinley, Theodore Roosevelt, William Howard Taft, and Vice President James S. Sherman. The spittoons were still there.

was estimated that 900,000 might be needed for the job. When bricklaying actually began in mid-September, 1885, *The Statesman* said that the appointment of Thomas Finnegan as foreman was a "guarantee that the work will be well and faithfully done." By mid-November the brick work was finished and the roof was being put on. Another month saw the painters at work. When the legislature convened that winter, it met for the very first time in a building especially designed for the functions of government.

All earlier legislative meeting halls had been merely rented, and on several occasions, even small retail stores had been used. The new building lent itself to all sorts of functions not envisioned by the planners. In 1892, for example, a grand Leap Year Ball was held in the "great corridor" on the second floor. The Senate chamber was used as a drawing room and for a musical program.

Before the cornerstone was laid, in the spring of 1885, one local wit suggested that the honor of laying it be given over to the "whiskey men" since the building was to be paid for mainly out of the whiskey tax.

Idaho Territory's new capitol looked like this when completed in 1886. Its grounds were unadorned with any tree or shrub, but its park-like setting would be lush by the turn of the century.

ISHS 187-1

The Overland House, northwest corner of Eighth
and Main, looked like this in the 1870s.

The Eastman Brothers, Hosea and Ben, enlarged
the Overland hotel in the mid 1880s. They
changed its appearance considerably by roofing
over the second story porch.

Historic Hotel

 "The Columbia Band gave a farewell concert last evening from the Overland balcony, concluding the program with *Auld Lang Syne*. As the closing strains of the famous old melody died away, the lights in the major portion of the Overland were turned off for the last time." With these words, *The Idaho Statesman* reported the nostalgic send-off that Boise City accorded one of her oldest landmarks on June 30, 1904. It was the custom in those more sentimental times to have pioneer get-togethers, banquets, and speeches to mark the passing of a particularly famous building. The Overland Hotel was one of these.

Built by B.M. Durell in the summer and fall of 1864, the Overland House, as it was then called, had its formal dedication on September 30, 1864. From the beginning it proudly advertised itself as Idaho's finest hostelry — a distinction not too hard to earn in the early years, when most accommodations available to travelers were primitive.

It stood on the corner of Eighth and Main, later site of the Eastman Building, and was long considered the very heart of the community's life and activities. Not only were most holidays celebrated at the Overland with banquets and balls, but it was where all of the stagecoaches arrived and departed. It is said that people would stay up until 2 o'clock in the morning just to see a stage pulled by six prancing horses wheel up to the Overland, whether they were meeting anyone on board or not.

In reporting a "bachelor's ball" held there in 1871, *The Statesman* quipped: "The sterner sex behaved well, although it cannot be said to have been a dry well." The bachelor's ball of 1868 had also inspired the reporter. He said, "If the turpentine isn't knocked out of 'them boards' tonight, we are no judge."

The success of the Overland, even though a number of other hotels were operating in the city, was shown by the constant need for additions to increase its capacity over the years. In 1878, it was described as "a building of magnificent proportions" with new brick additions.

In 1879, the Eastman brothers from Silver City, who were now its proprietors, built a two-story porch and balcony addition, making it a more impressive structure still. In 1884, this porch was further extended and remodeled. In 1888, a two-story brick building was added next door on Main Street.

OVERLAND CAF'E
OPEN DAY NIGHT.

This photograph of the pioneer reunion of June 29, 1904, records the passing of the historic hotel from the Boise scene. Demolition to make way for the big Overland (later Eastman) Building began soon after.

The best evidence we have for identifying this as the lobby of the Overland House is the wall clock at left, now in the collection of the Idaho State Historical Society. It is known to have hung in the famous hotel.

A number of prominent Idaho hotel men took their turns at managing the Overland, but the Eastman brothers, H.B. and Ben, retained control. In February, 1899, the first mention is made of a possible new building on the famous Overland corner. H.B. Eastman called a meeting of potential stockholders (the city's half dozen richest men), to consider his plans for a new hotel. The hotel was never built, however, for when plans for the new building were agreed upon in 1903, it was for an office block, four stories high, with retail stores on the ground floor. Construction was planned for 1904, and the doors of the Overland Hotel were closed to the public for the last time at 9 o'clock on the evening of June 28, 1904. On the following afternoon, all pioneers who had come to Idaho before 1868, were invited to "a farewell feast under the old roof."

The big, new commercial structure on the site of the historic hostelry, was called the Overland Building from its completion in 1905, until its enlargement in 1910. With the addition of two more floors, making it a six story building, the name was changed to the Eastman Building, and so it remained for another 40 years.

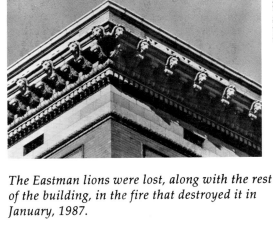

The Eastman lions were lost, along with the rest of the building, in the fire that destroyed it in January, 1987.

As completed in 1905, the Overland Building had four stories. Its Italian Renaissance terra cotta cornice, with more than a hundred lion heads, would be removed and reinstalled when two additional floors were added in 1910.

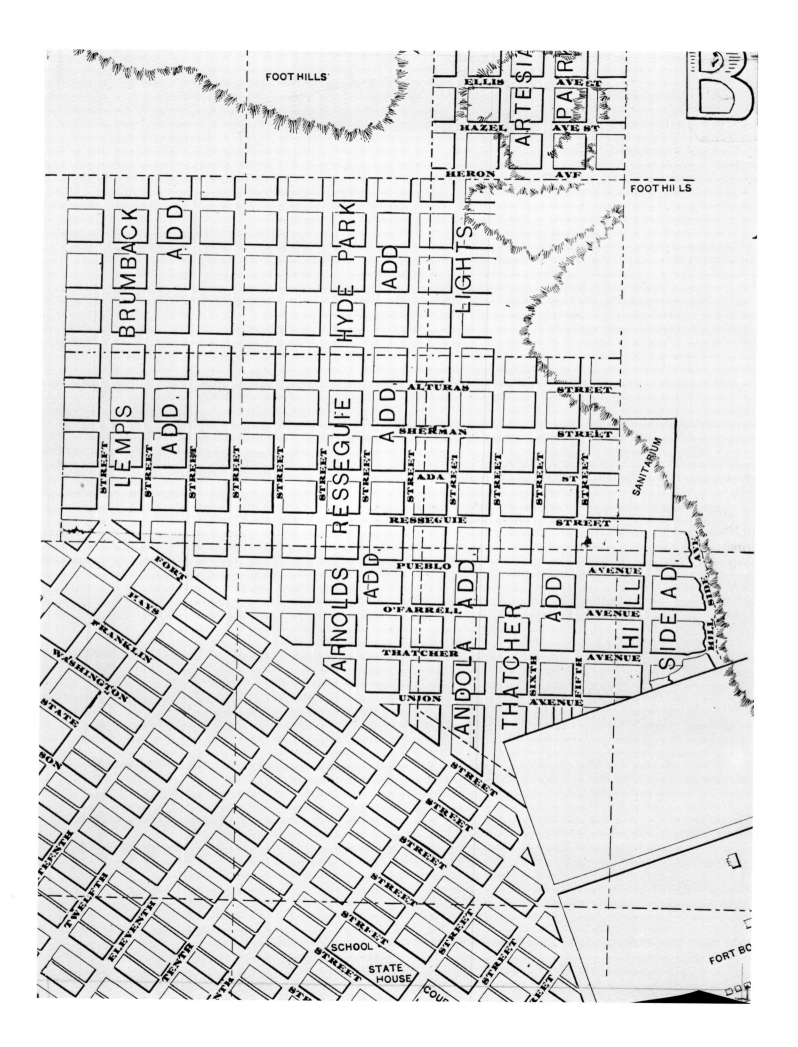

158

Growing by Addition

Old-time Boiseans had an awareness of "neighborhood" that has almost disappeared from the consciousness of more recent arrivals.

When someone mentions Central Addition, do you know immediately which part of the city is being referred to? How about Lemp's Addition? Although many Boiseans are aware that John Lemp was an important early citizen of the community, and that there is a Lemp Street and a Lemp's Apothecary even today, few can relate the name to a specific part of town.

Like most American cities, Boise grew through real estate developments actively promoted. One of the first real estate businesses to use imaginative and persistent advertising was that of Walter E. Pierce. It was he who first used large-sized display ads in the daily newspapers to publicize the new parts of town where lots were being sold and houses built. Pierce followed a consistent pattern of building a fine house for himself in each of these new developments — a house that he usually sold at a profit in a few years after the neighborhood was firmly established.

Idaho's long-time Governor's House, at 1905 North 21st Street, was one such Walter E. Pierce house, built in 1914. Pierce opened his real estate business in Boise in 1890, and from then on was in the thick of the "addition" business. It is from his firm's map of 1895 that we get the following list of real estate developments of that decade:

Andola's Addition was named for A.R. Andola, a real estate broker who had his offices downtown, and lived at Seventh and Jefferson. This neighborhood centers on Sixth from Fort to the alley beyond Pueblo. Arnold's Addition was the project of dentist Dwight Arnold. Dr. Arnold lived at 2042 North Thirteenth, and the property he developed extended from Fort to Resseguie, and from Ninth to Thirteenth. Brumback's Addition was one of the largest in the North End, embracing 32 city blocks from Eastman to beyond Irene, and from Thirteenth to Harrison Boulevard. Jeremiah Brumback was its original owner and promoter.

Bryon Addition was named for William Bryon, former sheriff of Ada County, who lived at 1419 North Eleventh. Thomas Donaldson, in his book on early-day Idaho, describes how Bryon was elected sheriff of the county in 1870, even though the first count left him one vote short. (It turned out that four black men had voted for him, but their votes had not been counted. When this was

Walter E. Pierce was Boise's great real estate promoter from 1890 until 1930. He and partners John M. Haines and L.H. Cox changed the face of the city with major residential and commercial developments.

Main Street, looking east, about 1892. John Lemp's big three-story brick building at right forms one of the anchors for the banner promoting Lemp's Addition in the North End. The Overland Hotel's two-story porch at the corner of Eighth shows at left.

called to the attention of an impartial judge, he declared Bryon elected by three votes). Bryon's Addition included the blocks bounded by Eastman, Ninth, Thirteenth, and the alley south of Lemp.

Central subdivision was one of the finest Victorian neighborhoods in the city, although in a location that was later cut off by industrial development. One of the finest mansions in that area was that of Judge George H. Stewart, at the corner of Myrtle and Fifth Streets. The big house is now divided into apartments. Altogether, Central Addition included the blocks between Third and Fifth, and Myrtle and the railroad tracks. Like other additions of the 1890s, it helped make Boise into a city of attractive residential neighborhoods.

The W.E. Pierce & Co. real estate office at the southeast corner of Tenth and Main was directly across from the Idanha Hotel, as the reflection in the window nicely shows. Left to right are partners Pierce, Cox and Haines.

What Time Is It?

Standard time zones for the world were not adopted until an international conference held in Washington, D.C. in 1884. At that time 24 zones were established with Greenwich, England, as the prime meridian.

Boise City, and many other places, did not immediately adopt the new system, however, continuing to favor "sun time." (When the sun was due south of where you happened to be, that was noon, whatever the longitude.) By sun time Boise and Portland are 25 minutes apart, but when Portland adopted standard time and Boise didn't, the two were only 15 minutes apart.

As if this wasn't confusing enough, American railroads had long had an even worse system. Each of more than 75 companies used its own "railroad time," based upon where its main office was located. After the Oregon Short Line reached southwest Idaho in 1883, Boise hotels and some businesses began to use two clocks, one set on sun time and the other on railroad time. When the railroad adopted standard time, the city stubbornly kept its sun time, and two-clock system.

Since Boise was placed in the Pacific time zone at first, the 25 minutes difference in sun time with Portland would have been eliminated, but even though many, including *The Idaho Statesman*, had urged adoption of standard time since 1887, it would be another ten years before the City Council passed an ordinance making it official.

Boise's post office and a number of businesses had gone on Pacific Standard Time on January 1, 1892, but there was still strong opposition, led by banker C.W. Moore. *The Statesman* said he was "one in a million" in fighting the new system.

When the Council did take action in 1897, it adopted Mountain Standard Time. All of southern Idaho then had one time, but North Idaho remained on Pacific Time, and still does. *The Idaho Statesman* was most unhappy with the decision, pointing out that "Mountain Time is 45 minutes too fast for this place." At least Pacific Time would be only 15 minutes slow, it reasoned.

In October, 1897, jewelers Hesse and Sturges erected a pole in front of their store near Eighth and Main Streets. It was to hold what was called by the paper "the new city clock." In December, with the big timepiece in place, *The Statesman* praised the enterprising merchants for their generosity in supplying the city what it had long lacked — a "public clock."

There was an earlier street clock near the spot where Hesse & Sturges put up theirs in 1897, as this 1889 view of Main Street shows. Frank Coffin's tin shop, at right, was replaced with the big, new Pioneer Block in 1894.

Boise City's "public clock" stood for many years just west of the corner of Eighth and Main. This view of about 1912 shows part of the Eastman Building in the background.

St. Michael's Episcopal church.

CIVILIZING INFLUENCES
The Sound of Bells

 James S. Reynolds, founder and first editor of *The Idaho Tri-weekly Statesman*, writing in April, 1869, complained that "Boise City is sadly in need of a church bell of some kind. Why don't we have one?"

By February, 1870, he was able to note "the bell for the Episcopal Church has arrived. It weighs four hundred pounds and will be put in position soon."

A few days later, while carpenters were putting the finishing touches on the wooden bell tower, Reynolds waxed eloquent and a bit nostalgic as he anticipated what a bell would mean to Boise: "It will be swinging in a few more days, when its sweet tones may be heard awakening the echoes of the surrounding country. It will be sweet music to many of us who have not heard the sound of a church bell for years."

This first church bell in Boise was referred to as "the Village Bell" in an account of its first ringing. This took place on Saturday, February 26, 1870. It was some time before other churches in the capital city had bells, and there is a curious thread of concern about this running through *The Statesman* for years. No doubt those early Idahoans, all of whom had grown up elsewhere, considered bells in steeples a mark of civilization, and were eager to have this frontier community acquire such civilizing attributes.

Of churches and religious activities there were plenty, however, even without bells. The first Catholic church was reported half-built by January, 1870, by soldier volunteers from Fort Boise. It was described as Gothic in style, 20x40 feet over-all. On Jan. 11, 1871, less than a year after its completion, it was totally destroyed by fire. The loss was about $8,000, and the building wasn't even paid for.

In May, Catholic services were being held in the house of John O'Farrell. Bishop Lootens and Father Mesplie officiated. By November, 1871, the Catholics, although "somewhat discouraged," were collecting pledges toward the building of a new church.

Father Mesplie had established the Catholic church at Idaho City in 1863, and had been in the Pacific Northwest for over twenty years by 1871, when he helped Boise Catholics get started on a new church to replace the burned one.

Other denominations were mentioned in *The Statesman* at an

ISHS 2128

St. John's Roman Catholic church, 1876-1905, replaced an earlier one destroyed by fire. It, too, burned in 1905, and was replaced by St. John's Cathedral, begun in 1906.

ISHS 76-37.75

The Baptist church at Ninth and Idaho was depicted in this 1884 lithograph. The Baptists didn't have a bell in their tower as late as 1891, and The Statesman *thought it a pity.*

ISHS 489-C

The Methodists' handsome brick Gothic church was built in 1875. It did have a bell soon after. It stood at the northwest corner of Eighth and Bannock where Hotel Boise was built in 1930.

early date. In May, 1871, three Methodist preachers from California set up a tent and held camp meetings in Boise that drew large crowds.

A social festival was given by the Baptists in 1872 to raise money for repairing their church, and later that year E.J. Curtis, Secretary of the Territory, brought an organ back from an eastern trip for the Presbyterians, who didn't get around to organizing until 1878. The dedication of Boise's first Presbyterian church building took place in July, 1881.

By 1891, there were still only three churches in Boise with bells, and *The Statesman* thought it a shame. The Methodists, Episcopalians, and Catholics had bells, but the Baptists, Presbyterians, and Seventh Day Adventists didn't. These were the only completed churches in town in 1891, but the Christian Church was being built at Fourth and Jefferson.

Pipe organs became important to Boise's churches after the turn of the century. St. Michael's carved-oak organ, which cost $2,000, was hailed as the largest in Idaho on September 1, 1904. The very next day, September 2, the Methodists announced that theirs had cost $4,000, had 963 parts, and had filled an entire railroad car. Both arrived in the same week.

Thomas Donaldson, in his classic reminiscence of Boise in the late Sixties and Seventies, recalled that first bell at St. Michael's very well. He also remembered the code that was used when it tolled the news of a death in the community. One stroke meant male, two, female, and after a pause, the age of the deceased was tolled out. Donaldson remembered one morning in front of the Overland Hotel, when every gambler present began to bet on the age of the departed citizen — real sports could gamble on anything in those days.

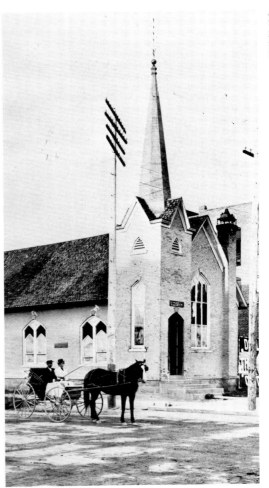

The modest brick First Presbyterian church at Tenth and Main was torn down in 1899 to make way for the Idanha Hotel. By then the denomination had a fine new church several blocks away. The Rev. and Mrs. J.H. Barton are in the buggy in foreground.

Boise's many saloons were part of an all-male world that no decent woman ever saw. This unidentified establishment was photographed in about 1910.

Crusade for Temperance

 A temperance lodge called the Independent Order of Good Templars was formed in Boise in February, 1868. After building a large meeting hall on Main Street in 1870, the Order continued to grow, attracting members from all walks of life.

Attorney Jonas W. Brown of Idaho City was the most frequent lecturer, giving a series on "The Social Evils of Intemperance" in 1871. Mrs. Carrie F. Young, who also had a reputation as an effective speaker on the subject, was invited to come down from Silver City in 1872 to address Boise audiences.

Undoubtedly the most dramatic convert to the temperance movement in the 1870s was famous United States Deputy Marshal Orlando "Rube" Robbins. Although there is no evidence that Robbins ever had a drinking problem (as Brown apparently did) he had certainly been involved in plenty of cases as a lawman where liquor was responsible for death and destruction.

Even before *The Statesman* reported on February 6, 1873, that the marshal had "experienced religion," he had formed "Robbins Encampment, Independent Champions of the Red Cross" and had been elected Eminent Counselor. Banker C.W. Moore was chosen Senior Champion.

On Sunday, February 9, 1873, Robbins was baptized by immersion in the Boise River before a large crowd. In March he was chosen president of the Methodist Sunday school, and when Robbins Encampment of the I.C.R.C. met that same month there were 115 members present. *The Statesman* hailed it as "the most flourishing temperance organization ever had in this city." Of the more than 600 members east of the Cascades, Robbins' group was easily the largest.

That Robbins continued his dedication to the temperance cause is shown by the fact that he allowed the Ensor Institute for curing alcoholism to move into his own home at 520 Idaho Street in November 1892. Only two days after the Institute moved in, unfortunately, a patient named "Pancake Bill" Nelson died of a "fit" brought on by delirium tremens.

Although many temperance people were as active as ever, and there were new organizations on the scene like the Women's Christian Temperance Union, in the Ada County elections of 1892, only 75 prohibition votes were cast out of a total of 2700.

Only one photograph of Rube Robbins showing him in uni-

Mr. and Mrs. Jonas W. Brown were leaders in the long battle for temperance. He was a lawyer and eloquent speaker, and she a gifted amateur artist.

The Woman's Christian Temperance Union fought long and hard to achieve Prohibition in Idaho. Nettie Chipp was president in 1916 when this photo was taken in the organization's Boise office.

form survives. From the date of this picture, and Robbins' apparent age at the time, it seems likely that he wears the costume of a Champion of the Red Cross.

Another photograph of Orlando Robbins (page 173), taken when he was seventy, shows him as he looked when he was making a living raising Idaho horses for the Eastern market, instead of chasing outlaws. Even then, he was still fighting "demon rum," as the temperance people called it.

That prohibition finally came in 1920 was a cause for rejoicing in the old temperance movement, even though the results were hardly satisfactory to anyone. Prohibition led to widespread lawbreaking by a large number of Americans who refused to accept it, and to the rise of gangsters eager to supply the lucrative demand for illegal liquor and to control its distribution.

The repeal of Prohibition in 1933 led to even great rejoicing by the masses of Americans than had the passage of the Eighteenth Amendment in the first place. New organizations have taken up the battle to fight alcoholism, but very few today think prohibition could succeed in a democracy.

Idaho got a Prohibition law in 1915. Those who had labored long for a dry state gathered around the desk of Governor Moses Alexander as he signed the bill. It went into effect in 1916.

Rube Robbins (right) in the uniform of a Champion of the Red Cross, poses with some Boise friends. Colonel John Green (left) wears his U.S. Army dress uniform.

A Man Called Rube

Orlando "Rube" Robbins was the kind of man who becomes legendary, even within his own lifetime. Dodge City had its Wyatt Earp and Bat Masterson, Deadwood its Wild Bill Hickock, but Boise and southern Idaho had Rube Robbins.

Unlike the others, his reputation has never been expanded by writers of fiction; nevertheless, he is fully as worthy of romantic treatment and in many respects had a more varied and interesting career than any of them.

The people who knew him certainly thought he was something special, and in all of the memoirs and newspaper accounts we have seen, nothing but praise was attached to his name. Here are some vignettes from the remarkable life of Idaho's most famous lawman:

From *The Idaho Tri-weekly Statesman,* August 29, 1882: "Deputy United States Marshal Orlando Robbins arrived in this city last night on the Overland Stage, with the notorious Charley Chambers in his custody. The pursuit and capture of Chambers is as great a credit to Rube as any of the many remarkable achievements of Western sheriffs and marshals. In 13 days, with nothing but the natural instincts of his business as an inducement, Marshal Robbins has traveled 1,280 miles: going night and day by the shortest routes, and liveliest conveyances to be obtained." Perusers of *The Statesman* for those years will find many such stories.

When there was a robbery or murder, Marshal Robbins started in pursuit, and within a week or two usually follows the report that he brought in his man; he rarely had to kill him, either.

One of the most famous Rube Robbins stories, told by such historians as former Governor Hawley and others who knew Robbins personally, deals with his duel with Egan, a chief of the Bannocks in the 1878 war. Accounts vary, but all agree that Egan recognized the famous Indian fighter at the battle of Silver Creek, near the mouth of the Owyhee River, and set out to take his scalp. Both men were mounted and armed with repeating rifles, and eye-witnesses were much impressed with the Indian's clever horsemanship. He would fire a few rapid shots, then drop down behind his horse's neck out of sight of his opponent.

Robbins got several bullet holes in his clothing and a scratch or two, but he shot Egan in the hand and body, knocking him off his horse before other Indians dragged him to safety.

ISHS 70-1.10

Rube Robbins was at the height of his powers and popularity when this portrait was made in 1879. That year he served as chief scout for the Army in the Sheepeater Indian campaign, and was Sergeant at Arms in the legislature.

Charles Ostner, pioneer artist, made this oil painting of Rube Robbins as a scout in the Indian wars of 1877-79.

Rube was easily Idaho's most famous scout in the Indian wars, serving as a captain of volunteers against the Nez Perces in 1877, as a colonel in the Territorial Militia during the Bannock War of 1878, and in 1879 was chief scout for the U.S. Army in the Sheepeater Campaign.

He also cleared up another "war" almost single-handedly when dispatched by Governor Ballard to Silver City in 1868, at the outbreak of hostilities there between opposing mining companies. This so-called Owyhee War had already resulted in two deaths when Robbins made a record six-hour ride from Boise and got the opposing factions to come to agreement and even to draw new deeds, all on the day of his arrival. When the governor arrived, everything had been pretty well settled by the ever-efficient Rube, although a later encounter on the street led to the death of prominent miner J. Marion More and one of his opponents in the dispute.

The versatility of Robbins is shown by the fact that he was elected to the Territorial Legislature in 1874-76, and served as Sergeant at Arms in 1879. His great talent, however, seems to have been law enforcement. From 1864, when he was a constable at Idaho City, until 1906, two years before his death, he was almost continually employed as a peace officer.

Whether subduing armed drunks on the streets of Boise, risking his neck stopping runaway horses, tracking Indians on the war path, or bringing back some of the most notorious stage robbers in Idaho history, Rube Robbins could always be counted upon to be cool, resourceful, and dedicated. If he knew fear, he never showed it.

How many men of 70 are still entrusted with the delivery of federal prisoners to the penitentiary? Rube Robbins was, only two years before he died.

ISHS 672

Even in old age Rube Robbins was a man to be reckoned with. He continued the fight for temperance and still took on hazardous law enforcement tasks.

Bishop Tuttle House, adjacent to St. Michael's Episcopal cathedral, honors the memory of the beloved early bishop.

Bishop Tuttle returned to Boise to dedicate Bishop Tuttle House in 1907.

Beloved Bishop

When the Episcopal Church decided to send its first bishop to the wilds of Idaho in 1867, the choice was an important and far-reaching one. Many an Eastern appointee to Idaho's frontier posts, including some governors, had been unpopular and ineffective because they were too "Eastern" in manners and tastes for the rough and tumble miners.

Daniel S. Tuttle, son of a blacksmith, was a big, hearty man who conveyed an impression of strength and confidence, and who turned out to be well-matched to the challenging and difficult job of frontier bishop. As Dick d'Easum points out in his 1964 centennial history of St. Michael's Cathedral, Tuttle had been a heavyweight boxer as well as a biblical scholar. He had the energy, courage, and sense of humor to persist in his mission, no matter how tough things got. In a letter to his wife, he described his introduction to Idaho:

"I arrived at Boise City Saturday afternoon, October 12, 1867, with a broken neck, bruised head, aching bones, sore throat, and disturbed temper . . . Of all the uncomfortable routes I ever traveled over, that from Salt Lake to Boise is the worst . . . for hundreds of miles you see no vestige of civilized man except at the stations, and the stock tenders kept by the stage company."

This experience on the Idaho desert would soon be a regular part of Tuttle's life as would his familiarity with Idaho's canyons, mountains, and forests, for in his nearly 20 years in the West, he traveled thousands of miles to preach in every remote mining camp and farming town.

Within a month the bishop had organized a parish school in Boise which gave instruction in many subjects besides religion. Classes were taught in the little church built in 1866 by the town's first Episcopal pastor, St. Michael Fackler. The school was so successful that a large wing was added to the church in 1869 with funds Tuttle had raised. The burly bishop helped build it with his own hands.

Educational opportunity was of great concern to Bishop Tuttle. He was appalled to find that Idaho City had no school at all when he first visited there. "This is a disorderly town," he wrote, and estimated that there were more Chinese living there than whites. For many years Tuttle's visits to Idaho City and Boise were reported favorably in the newspapers, since his sermons were

Bishop Daniel Sylvester Tuttle when he was missionary bishop of Idaho and a vast area of the West besides. His sermons were remembered for years afterward.

among the best those towns had a chance to hear.

When Bishop Tuttle left Idaho in 1887, to assume the position of Bishop of Missouri, he was one of the most widely loved and respected men who had ever lived in Idaho. He later was made presiding bishop of the Protestant Episcopal Church in the U.S.

Tuttle's place in American, as well as in Idaho history, was brought home to us a few years ago during a visit to St. Louis. Our wanderings brought us unexpectedly to the old Episcopal Cathedral of that city. The imposing building adjoining the cathedral itself had a familiar name: "Bishop Tuttle House." The fine oil portrait of the bishop in the hall confirmed indeed that it was the same big and hearty man with the bald head and full beard who had once been so widely known and respected by the people of Idaho.

ISHS 76-138.14

CULTURAL DIVERSITY
Oriental Presence

Although much has been written about Idaho's early-day Chinese, there are enough unpublished anecdotes and forgotten newspaper items to fill several fascinating books. If written with sensitivity, these will also reflect the loneliness and hardship that was part of Chinese life in a world dominated by white prejudice.

Even in the late 1860s when Chinese laborers began to arrive in Idaho in large numbers, there were a few isolated voices raised in behalf of fair treatment for the Orientals, but generally speaking, white miners regarded the Chinese as a serious threat to their own chances of making a living. It soon became apparent that the Chinese were willing to work harder on poorer claims than the whites, and for considerably less money. They also had an annoying habit of saving what they made. In fact, there wasn't much about the unoffending "Celestials" that didn't annoy most white miners considerably.

The list of crimes committed against Idaho's Chinese a century ago is depressingly long, and the list of convictions of whites guilty of such crimes remarkably short. Violence to Chinese property was often treated as a lark, and there are many accounts of even small boys throwing sticks and stones at Chinese as they passed down the streets of Boise — no doubt a reflection of attitudes learned at home. *The Idaho Tri-Weekly Statesman* usually deplored such acts, and asked that the parents of such boys administer suitable punishment.

The Chinese themselves came in for their share of criticism in the papers, especially for their use of opium. In 1871, *The Statesman* noted that "the China population are planting gardens here pretty extensively. They are so patient and puttering that they do well. If that was all they planted it would be all right." After a fire in Boise that same year, the paper had this to say: "Their lives are a debauch. They crowd together and drink and gamble all night, or steep their senses in the lethargy attendant on opium smoking, and these fires are the natural consequences."

After taking up occupations other than mining, the Chinese became a familiar part of life in most Idaho towns. "John China-man makes his appearance at our doors bright and early every morning with the traditional pole and baskets, the latter filled with every variety of fresh plucked and cool vegetables." There were many Chinese laundries and restaurants, and many fami-

ISHS 75-104.1

Boise's Hip Sing tong was one of several protective societies active in the city's Chinatown through the years. The Hip Sing building, near the corner of Capitol Boulevard and Front Street, lasted until 1971 when it was demolished by Urban Renewal.

Boise's Hip Sing Tong building was decorated
with red, white and blue bunting for the visit of
the organization's national president in 1927.
Mayor Walter F. Hansen is in center.

lies hired the hard-working Orientals for domestic servants.

In 1873, during Chinese New Year celebrations, it was noted that "many families have been rendered disconsolate over the absence of the cook and washer-woman from their posts of duty this morning. It takes a Chinaman a week to get his head into proper shape after a New Year's collarup, so the corner in cooks will continue for several days yet."

Chinese celebrations generally mystified and amused white citizens. There is much to suggest, however, that few people took the trouble to find out anything about Chinese culture. Certainly the language barrier was partly to blame. A rare exception is a note in 1882 that "the Chinese yesterday were celebrating the anniversary of the birth of a hero who flourished about 2000 years ago."

Chinese kites, looking like hawks, attracted considerable local attention, and Chinese firecrackers, a feature of all celebrations, including funerals, were part of the color in Idaho towns when Chinese were numerous. Many of Boise's older citizens can still recall Chinese parades, with prancing dragons and exotic music. They lent a richness and excitement to the lives of children especially, but the whole town turned out to enjoy the Oriental festivals of yesteryear.

ISHS 71-156.11

Chinese men of Boise often had families in the old country arrange their marriages. Lovely Greta Fong came to America to marry Harry Fong in 1927. Her wedding portrait was taken by Ansgar Johnson, Sr.

ISHS 76-114.6

Chinese gardeners were renowned for their skill. By the 1920s they were delivering produce door to door with Model T Ford trucks instead of with baskets on a pole.

C.K. Ah Fong was perhaps the ablest physician on the Idaho frontier. He treated both Chinese and Whites in Idaho mining camps from the 1860s on, using centuries-old techniques like acupunture and herbal medicines.

ISHS 81-2.32

Chinese New Year's, with its colorful parades and exotic music, was enjoyed by the whole town. The dragon, carried on the backs of several young men, was an especial favorite of the youngsters.

The Modern Hotel was one of many Basque boarding houses that helped make Boise "The Basque capital of America." This group was photographed there in 1926.

Basque Boarders

Boise's Basque boarding houses fulfilled a real need for hundreds of homesick young men from Spain in the early years of this century. Nearly all of them had come to Idaho to work as sheepherders, even though most had no experience at it. It was one of the few kinds of work that the first Basque immigrants had been able to find in the American West, and they did it so well and faithfully, that large sheep companies were willing to hire more of them.

Inability to speak English was not a handicap in sheepherding, as it was in many other kinds of work. If a young man from the old country was recommended to his boss by a friend or relative in Idaho, ranchers were willing to take a chance on him. Conscientious and reliable herders were in demand, since their performance could make the difference between a profitable season, or a disaster.

When they were not on the range with their flocks, camping out in covered wagons, Basque herders came to town to meet their friends, pick up their mail, and enjoy somebody else's cooking. The boarding house was ideal for providing a needed home base, and Boise was a big enough little city, with a growing Basque population, to supply what was needed.

By 1912, Boise's Basque community was well established. Some of the pioneers, like John Archabal, Benito Arregui, John Echevarria, and Juan Yribar were men of property. A 1916 Idaho gazeteer lists other Boise Basques who had started out working for somebody else, at low wages, but were now in business for themselves as wool growers: Aberasturi, Aciturri, Aldegocea, Andueba, Argachsa, Audiza, Calzacorta, Gabica, Mendiola, Navarro, Solosabel, Uberuaga, and Yriondo. (Some of these spellings are suspect, since directory compilers had trouble with Basque names. We have corrected those we could).

In 1918, Boise's Basque community was able to secure a Basque-speaking priest and establish its own parish. Father Bernardo Arregui came from Spain to minister to the people of the Church of the Good Shepherd at 420 West Idaho Street. (This building was the Roman Catholic Chancery for many years, and is now a law office.)

The numbers of Basque herders who lived in Boise's boarding houses, as listed in the old city directories, is quite astonishing, unless you realize that for many of them the house was little more

ISHS 72-90.1

By 1933, many Basque men who had started life
in the American West as lonely sheepherders,
had families and friends in well established
Basque colonies in Idaho towns. This happy
group is enjoying a picnic at Boise's Mode
Country Club in 1933.

than a mailing address for much of the year. When they did have time off, chiefly in winter, the boarding houses were packed, and social life was active. Good Basque cooking, wine, music, and lots of conversation helped make up for the lonely months spent out in the sagebrush.

Mateo Arregui's Modern Rooming House, at 613½ West Idaho Street, was the address of no less than 238 Basque herders in 1912. Obviously, only a few of them could sleep there at any one time, but for them, it was a "home away from home." Juan Anduiza's hotel, at 216 South 9th Street, had 42 listings in 1912. Anduiza had operated the City Lodging House on North 9th in 1909. In September, 1914, he secured the building permit for a new hotel and enclosed jai alai court at 619 Grove. Briggs & Associates, consulting engineers, now occupy this historic Boise landmark.

Antonio Letemendi was proprietor of the Delamar Rooming House at 807 Grove in 1912. The picturesque mansard-roofed mansion built by banker C.W. Moore in 1879, had become home to 43 Basque herders. It was still a Basque boarding house in 1970, shortly before its demolition.

ISHS 75-158.1

Antonia Ysursa, Carmen Luque, and Ecolastica Ondarza pose proudly in native costume, with the handsome flag Mrs. Ysursa made in about 1932 for the American Basque Fraternity Auxiliary.

The historic Delamar House, C.W. Moore's 1879 mansion, became thereafter, home of the Arid Club and a Basque Boardinghouse. It was torn down in 1972.

None of Boise's Basque boarding houses surpasses the little brick dwelling at 607 Grove Street for historic significance. It was built in 1864 by pioneer merchant Cyrus Jacobs, an imaginative and progressive businessman who showed the way in all kinds of community enterprises.

In addition to the general merchandise store he ran at the corner of 7th and Main Streets (where Idaho's tallest building now stands), Jacobs owned a gristmill near 13th and Main, where he used water power to grind local farmers' grain. With some of this grain he distilled a rye whisky that was famous in Idaho mining camps under the label "Jacobs' Best."

Other grain and the mash from the distillery were fed to Jacobs' hogs. In his packing plant Cy cured hams and bacon for wholesale distribution to other Idaho towns. When he started this branch of his business in February, 1868, *The Statesman* said he was making better bacon than any brought from Oregon — "nice, clean, fatted just enough and cured just right." He was processing two tons of ham and bacon per week and increasing that rate steadily. The paper thought this a great thing for Idaho, and estimated that Jacobs was saving consumers about $13,000 per week over what they had been paying for Walla Walla or Oregon bacon.

In August, 1868, Cyrus Jacobs was elected Ada County Treasurer and poured champagne for his friends at the Main Street store to celebrate. This was his earliest venture into local politics, but in 1879 he was elected mayor of the city. Jacobs' right-hand man in the early years was Charles Himrod. He, too, served Boise as mayor, in 1870 and again in 1878.

Like other Idaho pioneers, Cy Jacobs had passed through Boise Valley on the Oregon Trail before ever dreaming that he would one day settle there. The young man was in a wagon train headed west in 1852, when he first looked down from the bench south of town at the future site of Boise City. Aside from cottonwoods and willows along the river, and a fringe of fir trees along the summit of Boise front, he would have seen no other vegetation but sagebrush for miles, and not a single cabin.

The Jacobs' charming little brick house is shown on the next page with members of the Jacobs family posing in the yard at 607 Grove Street. More than 100 years later the house still looks

almost exactly as it did then, but it has seen a lot of history that doesn't show from the outside.

The Jacobs' circle of pioneer friends included William J. McConnell, elected Governor of Idaho in 1892. McConnell's attractive daughter Mamie had helped in his election campaign; it was then that she met a handsome young attorney, newly arrived in town from the midwest. His name was William E. Borah. In April, 1895, they were married in the parlor of the Cyrus Jacobs house before a few close friends.

Cy Jacobs died at the turn of the century. His widow, Mary Elizabeth, lived in the Grove Street house until her own death on February 18, 1907. By 1909, the little brick dwelling had become a boarding house. The city directory for that year lists Edward Fitzpatrick, cigar maker, and others as living there. Mrs. Ella Abbott lived at 607½ Grove, possibly in a building behind the Jacobs house.

Basque history in the Jacobs house began in 1910, when Mr. and Mrs. Simon Galdos ran it as a boarding house. Siriaco Bicandi was a later manager, before Joseph Uberuaga acquired the property in 1918. He and his family ran it as a boarding house for Basque herders for more than 60 years thereafter.

The Oinkari Basque Dancers of Boise have performed nationally. They are carrying on the rich traditions of their culture by training young people in music and dance.

GOLDEN AGE OF SPORT

Before a national radio network was established, huge crowds gathered in front of the Idaho Statesman building at Sixth and Main to read the latest bulletins as they were posted. It was here that people learned of the progress of Lindbergh's flight to Paris, got round-by-round accounts of championship prizefights, and inning-by-inning World Series scores.

A Wonderful Year

 The year 1927 was a memorable one for Boise. Not only did Charles A. Lindbergh make his trans-Atlantic flight and follow it up with a visit to the city, underlining the fact that the "air age" had arrived, but other things happened to make that year fun to recall.

In sports, the era has often been called the Golden Age. 1927 was the year Babe Ruth hit 60 home runs — a record that stood for over 30 years. The Yankees went on to win the World Series in four straight games from the Pittsburgh Pirates, led by their famed "murderers' row" of hitters.

In September, in Chicago, Gene Tunney decisioned Jack Dempsey in their re-match for the heavyweight title. It was the famous "long count" fight in which Dempsey failed to get a knockout because the timekeeper delayed the start of his count over the fallen Tunney, who then got up to win on points. A crowd estimated at 10,000 people jammed the intersection of Sixth and Main in Boise to hear the bulletins read from *The Statesman* office — a crowd representing half the population of the capital city. The young radio industry proudly announced that a record 55 stations had carried the fight, but it didn't do Boise any good.

Boise High School's amateur station KFAU was the only one in operation in this area in 1927, and it didn't have access to network programming or teletype. KFAU was on the air for an hour at noon and for a couple of hours in the evening, broadcasting agricultural bulletins and the rather limited music available to it. This was because most phonograph records were restricted for broadcast.

In the field of sport, 1927 was a good year for Idaho teams. The Coyotes of the College of Idaho had an undefeated football season under coach Anse Cornell, winning their second straight Northwest Conference title. College of Puget Sound lost to the Coyotes 14-6 on November 19 to close the season. That day was a big one for the Idaho Vandals, too. They beat Oregon State in Portland, 12-7, in a game that was so exciting that coach Charley Erb passed out from too much emotion. It took 15 minutes for his worried players to revive him. Idaho thus became a contender for Pacific Coast honors, only to be upset by Gonzaga later in the season.

A polio epidemic frightened Idaho enough in November that many public schools were closed for two or three weeks. Boise

The statue of Governor Frank Steunenberg that faces the capitol was unveiled in 1927. The Federal Building is at left, Pinney Theater in the background.

High was closed from November 9 until 28, but played its football games anyway. In defeating Gooding on the 24th, the Braves won the Southern Idaho title. In December, they played Moscow for the State Championship and won 27-0.

The face of Boise changed in 1927 rather noticeably: new buildings that year included C.C. Anderson's Golden Rule Store on Idaho Street (now the Bon Marche), S.H. Kress and Co., also on Idaho, and the Egyptian Theater on Main.

The statue of martyred Governor Steunenberg was dedicated in ceremonies before the Capitol in December. Memorial chimes at the new railway depot were also dedicated in 1927. The station itself had been built in 1925. Just as Boise was beginning to enjoy being on the Union Pacific mainline, it lost another form of transportation altogether. The last city streetcar ended its run at 12:20 a.m., June 15, 1927. Buses started running on city streets that same day.

Another vehicle often seen on Boise thoroughfares was the city's water wagon. It got into the news on June 11 by catching fire, of all things. This gave the reporters a chance for some fun. They solemnly asked the fire chief, "Any water burn up?" Chief Foster was equal to the occasion, however, replying "There was 30 gallons missing — figure it out for yourself."

Boiseans were thrilled and enchanted by the "glory of Egypt" as revealed at the opening of the Egyptian Theater in April, 1927. John Barrymore starred in "Don Juan." Architect Fritz Hummel designed the Egyptian Theater's magnificent interior details with the aid of books in Boise's Carnegie Library.

The Egyptian's exotic presence on Main Street was new to Boiseans when this picture was made in the late Twenties. The polychrome exterior and striped awnings have been restored.

Herb Lemp's Scrambled Eggs was considered by many the finest polo pony in America. Herb's fatal accident took place in practice, with another horse.

Capital Polo

When Boise old-timers get together, talk sometimes turns to polo. To newcomers, this is surprising, for they would hardly suspect that Boise was once the polo capital of the Pacific Northwest.

It is also hard to picture the old polo field today, because a number of buildings, including Boise Little Theater, now occupy much of its area.

Polo came to Boise when U.S. Cavalry troopers stationed at Boise Barracks began to play the sport in 1909. Since there was a long tradition in town of friendly rivalry between the "boys in blue" and civilian athletic teams, it wasn't too surprising that a civilian polo team was organized in 1910 to give the horse soldiers some competition.

That first team, which came to be known as Boise's "four horsemen," was to compile a remarkable record in the hard-driving, exciting, and dangerous game of polo. It consisted of Herbert Lemp, Ed Ostner, Harry Falk, and Charles Barringer. Substitutes included Romer Teller, Bill Jenkins, Chester Corley, and W.H. Estabrook of Idaho City. A polo club was also organized for the purpose of promoting the sport and arranging interstate tournaments.

Boise's team of Lemp, Ostner, Falk and Barringer played together for 17 years, taking on teams from Portland, Spokane, Ontario, and Seattle. They also played military teams from all over the west, sponsoring tournaments in the Twenties in which as many as eight teams came to Boise. Civilian teams from California also came, featuring Hollywood stars who were active in the game. Hal Roach and Guinn "Big Boy" Williams were among those who played in Boise.

In 1927, Herbert Lemp was elected mayor of Boise. The handsome Lemp, who had been captain of the Boise polo team since the beginning, promptly challenged another polo-playing mayor: Will Rogers of Beverly Hills. The Beverly Hills team was scheduled to come to Boise for the big northwest polo tournament when tragedy struck.

In a practice game, while riding a substitute pony named "Craven," Lemp was thrown and suffered a fatal head injury. He was sworn in as mayor while in the hospital, but died four days later.

A pall of gloom was thrown over Boise polo. In a touching tribute, Calvin Cobb wrote, "It seems to me that he should have been

ISHS 78-2.57

Boise's team of Glenn Balch, Chet Keltner, Luck Johnson, Art Fletcher and Bob Milan won the championship trophy in the 1932 spring tournament. Balch achieved national fame as a writer of children's books — mostly about horses.

ISHS 73-13.5

They called the little grandstand where wives and girl friends watched the polo matches "the crow's nest." This picture was taken in the 1920s.

saved to us. He always played the game cheerfully and so manfully. He was our boy." Another writer noted that "His enthusiasm, his dash, and his verve on the field often have rallied Boise against desperate odds for a final brilliant victory."

Mrs. Charles Barringer, whose husband played on the famed "four horsemen," recalled that the social life of Boise revolved around the polo field. She furnished the Idaho Historical Society with a collection of excellent photographs of those stirring days of Boise sport, including the one shown here of some polo wives at a match in the Twenties. In Mrs. Barringer's album this picture is labeled "The Crow's Nest," but those chic flappers hardly resembled crows.

Polo continued into the 1950s, with perhaps the greatest era of later days coming in the early Thirties. At this time Boise was represented by such fine players as Frank, Steen and Art Fletcher, Glen Balch, Lucky Johnson, Chet Keltner, Joe Rogers and Bob Milan.

John Rothchild was a member of the 1931 Company E, Idaho National Guard team which included Balch, Keltner, and Johnson. They defeated a 12-goal team from Santa Barbara that year. In 1954, John Barringer, son of "four horseman" Charles T. Barringer, played for a Boise Team in one of the capital city's last matches.

Boise women played polo, too. This is the Boise Ladies' Polo Team of 1926 — hey day of the sport.

ISHS 62-20.12229/a

*This great action shot was made in 1912 when
Boise played Ontario.*

*Boise's great "Four Horsemen" played together
from 1910 until 1927. Left to right: Herbert
Lemp, captain; Harry Falk, Ed Ostner and
Charles Barringer.*

Herbert E. Lemp, captain of the Four Horsemen, was a fine polo player. His Barrymore profile and personal charm made him a Boise favorite. His death in 1927, after he had just been elected mayor, was a community tragedy.

ISHS 69-81.41

Croquet was a gentle sport compared to others pioneer women and girls indulged in. They were not afraid to tackle more vigorous games, despite the obvious handicap of long skirts and high-button shoes.

Girls at Play

 Little girls in early Boise did much more than "sit on a cushion and sew a fine seam." Like their brothers, they were much more likely to lead the strenuous life of frontier children, both working and playing hard. If they were at any disadvantage in games with the boys, it was in clothing styles they had to wear.

In February, 1870, it was reported that "the schoolboys have introduced on their playground the game of shinny. Each player is armed with a big club, a ball is put upon the ground and at a signal, they all strike at it like they are mad. Its excellence consists in the number of times one boy can miss the ball and hit the next player on the shins. The one that can show the largest area of barked shins at the end of the game is counted big medicine. It is of frequent occurrence that a boy is seen with his legs wound about with rags like the bandaged limb of an injured cherry tree. The game is not fashionable with the girls — because they don't have any shins to bark." (Referring, no doubt to their long skirts.)

Shortly after, it was noted that the girls had taken to stilts. "They back up against a house, fence, or anything for a boost, mount the poles, and walk off like mad. They never ask a man to make a pair of stilts for them, but do their own carpentering in the back yard, using a smoothing iron, or a big rock to drive nails with." The reporter, evidently a rather young man, was captivated with the way the girls fell off their stilts, "a sort of triangular mass of beauty, curls, high heels, and so forth," but also reported the pungent comment of "an old bachelor" who said that "girls on stilts look like sandhill cranes hunting frogs on a rainy day."

Surprisingly enough, some of the young women apparently played football, too, a game much like the soccer of today. "The game of the period in Boise City is that of football. When the whole population, male and female, old, young, grave and gay, reverend and profane, get together with two footballs in the air, or bounding from the head of some unlucky passerby, they can shame the wild Indians with their yells and shouting, and have more genuine fun than anybody this side of Spider Creek . . .".

Later in the spring, it was noted that "the girls are giving up the ancient and graceful game of hop-scotch, and taking to the more refined and modern one of croquet."

Among winter sports, skating was popular. "Several ladies are learning to skate out at the park. It is said that the fair creatures

take to it as naturally as ducks to water, and consider it perfectly splendid." Roller skating was also available indoors in January of 1872, and the editor expressed the opinion that "Every lady ought to be a good skatist." He further advanced the rather frightening theory that "nine-tenths of the ladies of our cities lose their health, and die young, because they do not take sufficient exercise."

As early as 1869, there were reports of homemade bicycles running in Idaho. They were called "two-wheeled velocipedes," and anybody who rode one was considered a bit crazy. There is no reference to young women trying that dangerous sport yet, although by 1890, it was popular everywhere.

Courtesy Dale Walden

ACKNOWLEDGEMENTS

 The author wishes to acknowledge a number of people who made this book possible. First, the Board of Directors of Home Federal Savings who generously agreed to underwrite its publication and to dedicate all proceeds to three Boise non-profit organizations: Boise Senior Center, Boise Public Library Foundation, and Ronald McDonald House. Michael Koloski, vice president of Home Federal, worked with a committee created and led by Salle C. Schaffner of Boise City Celebrations to bring the project to fruition. John Head of Taylor Publishing Company has been helpful to the committee and the author at every stage.

My special thanks go to *The Idaho Statesman*, publishers of my weekly newspaper column on Idaho history for the past nineteen years, and to my friends at the Idaho Historical Library and Archives for their generous assistance: Judith Austin, M. Gary Bettis, Guila L. Ford, Elizabeth Jacox, Larry Jones, Marjorie Williams and John Yandell.

Merle Wells, most authors' final authority on the history of Idaho and the West, has contributed more than any one individual to my understanding of the broad sweep of Boise history.

Many of the photographs in this book were collected originally by Dale Walden of Boise. Over many years Mr. Walden has enriched the Idaho State Historical Society through generous sharing of his photographs, artifacts and knowledge. His contributions are much appreciated.

Duane Garrett, another respected friend, produced the prints of historic photographs that illustrate *Life in Old Boise*. His skills are widely known and much admired.

Finally, I owe special thanks to my wife Novella Dee, who spent several months typing and editing the book, and made many valuable suggestions.

Arthur A. Hart